In Balanchine's Company

BARBARA MILBERG FISHER

In Balanchine's Company

A Dancer's Memoir

Wesleyan University Press
MIDDLETOWN, CONNECTICUT

Published by Wesleyan University Press, Middletown, CT 06459
www.wesleyan.edu/wespress
Printed in the United States of America
5 4 3 2 1

The author gratefully acknowledges permission to reproduce the following:

Verse lines from "Among School Children," by William Butler Yeats, reprinted
with permission of A. P. Watt Ltd on behalf of Michael B. Yeats.

Lines from "The Idea of Order at Key West" and "The Planet on the Table," by
Wallace Stevens, reprinted by kind permission of the Knopf Publishing Group,
and courtesy of Peter Reed Hanchak, Executor, Estate of Wallace Stevens.

*Allegro Brilliante, Symphony Concertante, Firebird, Orpheus, Divertimento No. 15,
The Four Temperaments, The Nutcracker, Ivesiana, Agon,* © The George Balanchine
Trust. BALANCHINE is a trademark of the George Balanchine Trust.

Chapter 1 and portions of chapters 3, 11, 12, and 18 were published in *Ballet Revue*
(Fall 2004) and *Dance Chronicle* (Fall/Winter 2005). Chapter 12 first appeared in
Global City Review.

All efforts were made to locate the copyright holders for the images used in this
book.

Frontispiece: George Balanchine (mid-1950s). Photographer unknown, author's
collection.

Library of Congress Cataloging-in-Publication Data

Fisher, Barbara M. (Barbara Milberg), 1931–
In Balanchine's company : a dancer's memoir / Barbara Milberg Fisher.
  p.   cm.
Includes bibliographical references and index.
ISBN-13: 978-0-8195-6807-6 (cloth : alk. paper)
ISBN-10: 0-8195-6807-4 (cloth : alk. paper)
1. Balanchine, George. 2. Dancers—United States—Biography. I. Title.
GV1785.A1F57   2006
792.8'2092—dc22   2006004524

For Alice and Leonard

True genius doesn't fulfill expectations, it shatters them.

—Arlene Croce

O body swayed to music, O brightening glance,
How can we know the dancer from the dance?

—William Butler Yeats

Contents

x | Contents

Foreword

ARLENE CROCE

I celebrate the life of the dancer. She starts her training early. At eleven or twelve, she possesses the kind of body, ease of coordination, and elegance of bearing that immediately make her the envy of all who look upon her, and their mothers. She does not go through an awkward age. She does not get fat. She quickly becomes independent: she can be a fully fledged professional, with a paycheck, before she is out of her teens. If she is good enough to join one of the top companies, she gets to travel the world free and go to foreign-embassy parties, where she is received with honor as a representative of her country. (This was especially true during the Cold War, the time-frame of this book.) Finally, when she retires, she is still young enough to get married or start a new career.

This perfect life, as I see it, is exemplified in the life of Barbara Milberg Fisher. I should wish to have led it—provided, of course, I could still have had my own life in the end. And provided I'd had the talent in the beginning. To have spent one's youth dancing in the greatest of American companies, even if that were all that Barbara Milberg Fisher ever did, would be a major achievement. How it happened, the who-when-where, is not something she dwells upon here; it is for us to infer the unique combination of the historical and the personal—the gift of fortune that led her to Ballet Society just as it was being formed, and the gift of a dance talent musical by nature, bolstered by years of training as a classical pianist (oh, to be a pianist!). And that is how Barbara became a dancer of value to George Balanchine.

She danced for Balanchine during one of the most productive periods of his life and, after polio struck his wife Tanaquil Le Clercq, one of the most catastrophic. It is my loss not to have known the company well at that time. I could barely tell one dancer from another. When I saw Barbara in the original cast of *Agon*, it was without realizing precisely who she was—without realizing anything, really, except that, in this latest of Balanchine's creations with Stravinsky, I was witnessing something historic. It is amazing how fast the current was moving in the late fifties. Before I had a chance to form an adequate impression of Milberg's dancing, she had left the company, and what did she do but join Jerome Robbins's newly assembled Ballets: USA, surely one of *his* peak creations.

But all this is me peering in from outside. What the life and times of a dancer were actually like, only she can tell. She has her dinner-table stories (and there are some hot ones), and no doubt she has her regrets, but the equanimity with which she writes of herself as a typical young dancer of the fifties tells us that they are of little consequence in a much longer life of accomplishment. Barbara Milberg gave up dancing at the age of thirty-one, had children, and launched another career fully as demanding as dance but in no way touching it. When we met, she had been for a number of years a distinguished member of the faculty of the City College of New York, a teacher of English literature, and a scholar who had written to acclaim on Milton, Henry James, Borges, and Wallace Stevens. In this memoir, she concentrates on Balanchine, who has quite obviously continued to provoke her thought. She takes us back to a precious golden age in New York cultural history, the era of the "extended by popular demand" seasons at the City Center and the triumphant tours abroad. No one, I think, has evoked so well the camaraderie of company life in the years when American ballet was struggling for world recognition. Morale was at an all-time high, and it showed. Think of *Symphony in C* at curtain rise: the lovely bodies motionless but energized, ready to begin. As Milberg puts it here, "Never again would I feel such a charged, all-engulfing sense of purpose."

Although she long ago gave up the dancing life for the life of the mind, although her personal life has been a rich one, and her academic achievements are a matter of record, one feels that, for Barbara Milberg Fisher, nothing supersedes the memory of once having been part of a magic circle. That memory is the treasure she imparts to us now.

Acknowledgments

A memoir, it turns out, is all about other people. And a book of recollections with George Balanchine as its central focus will touch on a lot of other people—management, stage crew, wardrobe personnel, conductors, composers, musicians, designers, costumers, teachers, other choreographers, old cronies, and generations of dancers. Such a project consults extant memoirs and biographies; it reflects the work of scholars and librarians, has recourse to critical writings and reviews, profits from the laborious assembling of archives and special collections. For me, the richest outside source has been the extraordinarily vivid memory of dancers I worked with so many years ago. I should like to thank them, along with colleagues, friends, and various specialists who, over a period of years, helped to infuse this endeavor with some measure of heart, muscle, and accuracy.

Vida Brown Olinick, dancer, Ballet Mistress, friend, contributed generously and perceptively, with an exquisite eye for detail. Among other dancers whose memories might shame an elephant are Melissa Hayden, Ann Inglis, Una Kai, Robert Barnett, and Roy Tobias—the last two graced with simply phenomenal recall. Early on, both Barbara Walczak and Edward Bigelow kindly took the time to clarify ambiguities and share information, while Allegra Kent lightened my labor with humor and authorial understanding.

Barbara Horgan, whose close association with Balanchine spanned decades, was able to provide the perspective of management on several episodes that occurred in the fifties. I owe a special debt of gratitude to Madeleine Nichols, Chief Archivist at the Dance Division of the New York Public Library for the Performing

Arts at Lincoln Center, who shepherded my chosen illustrations through a labyrinth of permissions and copyright requirements. Many colleagues contributed to the manuscript. Patrick Cullen and Lucy Rosenthal offered stylistic and practical suggestions; Laury Magnus patiently heard chapter after chapter as each was completed and occasionally "tweaked" something into place with her usual critical acumen. My colleague, Linsey Abrams, arranged readings at the City College that helped tremendously in shaping the narrative; Ellen Ervin gave the manuscript an appreciative critical reading; Kathleen McCann and Grace Brophy, graduate school buddies, encouraged me throughout and threatened to turn the whole thing into a TV series. Gifted computer artist, Todd Patterson, took time from a crowded schedule to bring new digital life to a number of illustrations; and my daughter, Alexandra Fisher, helped bring this book to birth in a myriad practical ways, but also lent her lively intelligence to matters aesthetic.

My friend Judy Collins quietly did some practical research on my behalf, which led me to William Clark, a very special agent who seemed both delighted and amused to represent a dancer who was also a Wallace Stevens specialist. At Wesleyan University Press I found Eric Levy, my savvy editor, who has proven nothing less than a godsend: quick as Mercury, crystal clear in explanation, flexible in thought, firm in decision, sympathetic in understanding. A wise guide at the helm.

Perhaps this memoir would never have come into being without the encouragement of Allan Mandelbaum, poet, scholar, translator of Virgil and Dante, distinguished professor, polymath, lover of the city of Firenze—and my dissertation advisor. But for his immense learning, I should probably not have been introduced to the thought of many philosophers, theologians, and critics— or known the poetry of Osip Mandelstam. Through my years in graduate school he urged me to write about the time I spent in Balanchine's company. So this memoir is spiritually dedicated to Professor Allen Mandelbaum.

In Balanchine's Company

Prologue

ACH YEAR we collect at the top of a mountain in North Carolina over a long summer weekend. It began nearly a decade ago, and by virtue of common consent and our hosts' native generosity it has become a tradition. An informal annual reunion. Bobby and Ginger have been preparing for a week, cooking, arranging who will sleep where, planning side trips, putting everything in order. Bobby has just returned home after teaching a summer course in Fairbanks, Alaska. I've flown in from New York to find Ginger patiently awaiting my flight at the Asheville airport. Along with a change of clothes and a half-read murder mystery, I'm carrying chapters of my manuscript to read aloud. The people gathering at the Barnetts' mountain eyrie are among the few I can rely on to fill in information, help get my facts straight. And none of them are shy about setting me straight. Annie and Una have driven up from Savannah. Una emerges from the car with Luther, the cat who adopted her and refuses to be left behind. Annie walks toward the house carefully bearing a large white cardboard box, a monster cheesecake she has made. Others are already here: Todd, from Kansas City; Melissa, from Winston-Salem; Casey, from Columbia, South Carolina; Ronnie from Augusta, Georgia. The numbers vary from year to year. This August weekend, Vida and Helen will be coming to join us for the first time.

It's an enormous many angled house built of stucco, cedar wood, and stacked stone. Perched at the top of a mountain road, it has gardens, a courtyard with a fishpond and a little crossover bridge, and there's a deck off the kitchen where hummingbirds hover, sucking from vials of sugar-water. Down the hill, at the edge of the gardens, a stand of bamboo grows thicker and taller each year. A broad deck the width of the house extends from the living room, overlooking the mountain range. You can sit quietly out there and read, or look at the Smokies and listen to the birds. I go to the room I'm sharing with Annie and see treetops out one window, a bluish vista of peaks out the opposite side. I'm already planning to gather a few roadside flowers to put in the window. We hear a car approaching, the scrape of tires on gravel, and hurry out to greet the newcomers. They've been close friends their whole lives, these two: Vida, now living in Washington, D.C., and Helen, migrating between New York City and Florida.

It's going to be an interesting weekend. Walks around the grounds, up mountain paths hedged with pink crown-vetch, fragrant with sassafras; down the steep and winding access road with its several waterfalls; a visit to nearby Waynesville for shopping, or maybe Asheville. On the drive to Waynesville, my companions never fail to point out the country church that I once thought housed a strange congregation. On its pediment runs the legend I misread, originally, as "The Allen Greek Baptist Church." Are there Greeks here? Greek Baptists!? They broke up. It's Allen CREEK Baptist Church! Mild hooting and laughter. I get even as we're crossing Allen's Creek. Tell them I've thought of a terrific name for our little collective. You've heard of Elder Hostel? Yes, of course. Well *we* can start Elder *Brothel*. Make millions.

We spend our weekend at the Barnetts "dishing" (gossiping) and catching up on each others' lives. We pass around snapshots, talk of children and grandchildren, marriages, divorces, illnesses, accidents, deaths; compare weight loss, weight gain, travels, teaching, students who are doing well, students who are not performing or gone into some other line of work, as I have. We dine well. We love to eat and have educated palates—although Todd selects only salads. We summon up memories of precious time spent together many years ago, argue, laugh to the point of helplessness at long-gone disasters—the more disastrous they were, the funnier they are now—indulge in oft-repeated "Do you remember when . . . ?" stories, and generally bask in the ease that comes when you've known each other for a long, long time. Our backgrounds are diverse; our ages range over some thirty years. We are—we were—all dancers. Corps de ballet, soloists, and one or two, like Todd and Melissa, principal dancers. Several had toured with more than one ballet company, and a few had also worked in musicals. Vida and Una became ballet mistresses, Todd a respected choreographer. We will disperse in every direction when the weekend is over, go back to our private lives. But we meet together over a long summer weekend because we all danced with Balanchine. We came to know one another in Balanchine's company. We danced with Balanchine when the New York City Ballet was new. When NYCB was a phenomenon exploding into being against all odds.

I was never supposed to become a dancer. They had me slated for a Phys-Ed instructor (at least you get a pension) and hoped my brother David would eventually take over the practice. Dad was a dentist, Mom a hygienist with her own office and equipment. We lived on the first floor of a six-story building at the corner of Ocean Avenue and Dorchester Road in Brooklyn, and my parents' offices were adjacent to our living quarters. There was a private entrance for patients from the hall; another door gave access to our apartment; inside, a third door separated office and home. The neighborhood was quiet, the streets tree-lined, and my school within easy walking distance.

I was one of those skinny brats who absolutely cannot sit still. No *sitzfleisch*, they murmured. Nowadays it would probably be diagnosed as Attention Deficit Disorder, but I just liked to run around. Climb on chairs, over gates, up trees, jump puddles. See if I could clear the hedges outside our building. My arms and legs were mapped with scratches, scabs, black-and-blue patches earned by miscalculation or carelessness. When I got too rambunctious or invaded the office while a patient was in the chair—strictly forbidden—they told me to go practice the piano. My brother who was five years older had already learned to play, and in time I too was given lessons. These were Depression years, and the lessons were generally contracted by barter: dental work for piano lessons. And despite the strain on the family exchequer, I was also taken to ballet classes. The exercise was supposed to dissipate my nervous energy and curtail an unholy tendency toward mischief. But primarily I was given dance lessons to "build me up," because by the age of six I had nearly died twice.

When I was four, a galloping dysentery reduced me, I was told later, to fifteen pounds. My mother lived and slept in the hospital room, oversaw the hundred diaper changes daily, held my hands during blood transfusions, and fed me tiny portions of finely chopped raw apple, the only thing I was allowed to eat. At one point during all this, I saw my mother's curly blue-black hair turn white on one side of her head, and over a period of months grow in gray, then black again. A year later I contracted a virulent pneumonia. This was before sulfa drugs were on the market, and well before the discovery of penicillin. The fever built to a "crisis" and you either died or survived. I was housed in an oxygen tent, underwent an operation to facilitate lung drainage—my heart had been pushed to the right by an accumulation of unsavory matter—and got through another lengthy hospitalization. I made a near-miraculous recovery. But from that time on, at least according to my brother, I functioned as a walking, breathing, attention-getting mechanism invariably allowed to "get away with murder." And pig-headed into the bargain.

My big brother beat up on me regularly. Of course I provoked him beyond restraint. And I have to admit that, in later years, it was David who introduced me to Beethoven and Bartok quartets, which he played over and over until I could whistle passages from memory. And it was my brother's love of music that made me familiar with works of Hindemith, Webern, Shostakovich, and Stravinsky. Bach I got on my own. And he should never have locked me into the closet with the Bruckner Ninth Symphony at full blast from the speakers inside, when I'd only sneaked in to surprise him!

We all played chess—but Mom could beat everyone else in the family. My brother was captain of the chess team in high school, and my father was no slouch either, but Mom played a wicked game. She was a born strategist and she was tough. I remember coming home at times to find an intense, silent battle in progress. But I recall most vividly the first time I lost to her. She'd taught me all the moves as soon as I could learn them and had always let me win—until I turned twelve. I guess she thought I was old enough now to start learning the game for real and she trounced me in short order. It couldn't have been more than four or five moves before I heard a distinct "checkmate!" signaling the end of childhood. In a fury of shock and shame I sprang up, overturned the table scattering chess pieces all over the carpet, and bolted.

Our parents were Russian Jews who had been born in the Ukraine, not forty miles apart, during the last years of the 19th century. My father had attended Gymnasium in Odessa, unusual for a Jewish boy at that time, and along with Yiddish, English, and Hebrew (and a smattering of French and German) he spoke a fluent educated Russian. He left Russia at the age of seventeen, came alone to the United States in 1909, and was met at the docks in New York by his only relative in America, Uncle Philip from Philadelphia. This near-mythic personage—heard of but never seen— took the young immigrant under his wing for his first weeks here. Dad worked at the jobs he could get; he learned how to cut garments in a clothing factory, did heavy loading at the Post Office, and studied English at night school. He did military service during the First World War; made it through college, pre-med, and three years of medical school, and earned his dental degree at NYU. He shared a practice at first with another dentist—which is where he met and then married my mother, their hygienist. Sometimes Mom would tease "Doc" (my dad) by announcing that she should have hooked up with Dr. Hutchinson.

My plump little blue-eyed mother grew up in a tiny *shtetl* near Odessa. She remembered being punished, as a child, for licking a lime-coated wall (it turned out she had a bad case of rickets and desperately needed calcium). She also recalled how *her* father had carried her to the rich man's house in the village when she was very young, and held her up so that she could touch the miraculous electric light bulb, light without flame. Wasn't it hot!? No, she told me with a little laugh, it couldn't have been more than 15 watts. My maternal grandfather, after whom I was named, was a self-educated man. He tended the small grocery store in the village and ran an even smaller informal school on the side. The family name was Marantz but he was called Beryl Schreiber—Beryl the Writer—and when people needed letters written they would go to him. At the age of thirteen he was married to my grandmother, who was fifteen, by prearrangement, although they were not allowed to live together for two years. Grandma remained strictly orthodox and he remained a freethinker, which did not stop them from having seven children, five of whom survived. My mother was the oldest. She told me my grandfather tried unsuccessfully to teach her Latin when she was four years old and, disappointed, gave up on her as a future scholar. But I suspect he taught her chess.

I never knew my mother's father, who died of cancer at the age of forty-seven before I was born. Family legend has it that years after they moved to America, and two of my uncles were attending Cooper Union—one for Engineering and the other Accounting—they would sometimes get stuck on the math homework. What's the problem? Oh Pop, you wouldn't understand. Try me, he'd say, and they'd lay out the problem. According to both my uncles, hardly had they finished explaining when he'd come up with the solution. He couldn't say by what means he'd arrived at the answer, but when they worked it out they found he was correct. Always. How did you get that, Pop? And like the old joke, he would shrug, open his palms outward and declare "It was evident."

I studied piano with Dorothy who had beautiful eyes, pale skin, and long dark hair, carefully coiled; and I took ballet classes with Miss Selma who was blond, energetic, and very trim. My piano teacher lived upstairs in our building and I had a lesson every week. She paid strict attention to tone and phrasing, to the carriage of the hands, the rhythmic consistency of a trill. She'd play a bit of something she wanted me to learn so I could hear how it sounded, and point out how differently one approached a Mendelssohn rondo, a Beethoven sonata, a Bach fugue. With this teacher the music came alive; it took on drama, depth, a subtle coloration. This was the period of the Second World War and there was a framed photograph of her husband "Hershey" in uniform in the living room. (Many years passed before I discovered that my attractive piano teacher was the same Dorothy Taubman who taught Master Classes at the 92nd Street Y. There was the poster on the building announcing the classes, with Dorothy's face, but the long black hair had turned silver.)

I was supposed to practice for an hour every day after school, but of course I couldn't sit still that long. I'd charge out of the room periodically to check the wall clock in the kitchen. My parents set an alarm clock on the piano, locked me in, and went back to their patients. So I pushed open the window behind the piano, climbed down the iron gate that stood just outside in the courtyard, collected my little gang, and sallied forth to wreak mischief around the neighborhood.

When my dad first took me to watch class at Miss Selma's School of the Dance—I was somewhere between eight and nine years old—I became so excited they had to hold me down. It "took" instantly and I wanted to try everything I saw right away. Eventually they loosed me into an empty room where, tremendously stimulated, I bounced and spun, leapt about and fell down until my dad collected me to go home on the Flatbush Avenue Trolley. I loved dancing and performed constantly, in the schoolyard at P.S. 139 where I bumped into people, in the living room at home where I bumped into furniture, and in the courtyard of my building when I sneaked down the gate under the window and set the neighborhood kids twirling until they were dizzy. I ignored the scoldings of the more elderly tenants and my brother's unsolicited opinion that I was a royal nuisance. After a couple of years though, Miss Selma announced she was planning to marry and would be closing the school. I was devastated. But she told Mom that I "had something" and should try for the School of American Ballet, even if it meant taking me into Manhattan.

It was around this time that I was given *Little Women* as a birthday present. It was my first real book and I read it cover to cover maybe four times without a stop. When my brother and I were younger, Dad told us bedtime stories. Some were tales from the old country and some were original fabrications. My father was a marvelous storyteller, and I begged him again and again for the tale of the Poor Fisherman and the Magic Goldfish, or the one about Babayaga the Witch, who lives in a house that stands on three chicken feet. Best of all, though, was a saga entitled "Big Sister and Little Brother," a hilarious ongoing series in which a complicated prank is plotted, nearly abandoned, but at last triumphantly perpetrated by one of the siblings in return for the humiliation sustained in the previous episode. Even David was not too old to enjoy these "I'll-get-even" stories with their genius twist— the gender/age switch. Even vicarious retribution is sweet!

During the time between my father's stories and the gift of Alcott's *Little Women* I'd absorbed nothing but comic books, buying the most recent number with my weekly ten-cent allowance and then exchanging my new one for three used issues, and so on. I was deep into the adventures of Batman and Robin, Superman, Wonder Woman, and Captain Marvel (who was really the newsboy Billy Batson after he pronounced the magic "SHAZAM!"). Mom and Dad both found this literature distasteful and it was explicitly proscribed. So I cached my comic books safely away and was regularly reduced to consuming the tales under the covers with a flashlight after I'd been sent to bed. Louisa May Alcott accomplished what my parents could not. With the advent of the March sisters, I became a voracious general reader and abandoned outdoor shenanigans.

Now I couldn't be dislodged from the chair in the living room and started swiping books from my brother's small library whenever he left the house. The novels of Jack London, hardcover, each with its blue and white jacket: *The Call of the Wild, The Valley of the Moon, The Sea-Wolf, Martin Eden.* I raided the adult bookcases, took Fritz Wittels' *Freud and His Time* along to school one day hoping to scandalize or impress somebody (although the title was the only thing I was sure I understood). They introduced me at this point to the Brooklyn Public Library, a treasure house. I carried home armloads of treasure on the Flatbush Avenue Trolley. I was swept into worlds of fiction, lived in them. I wept over poor Elsie Dinsmore's motherless plight, her father so remote, absent on his business affairs until she suffers a near-lethal "brain fever." There was the multi-volume series detailing the experiences of Paul and Gabriel, brothers who attend an Episcopal boarding school (Paul is heroic, the noble-hearted captain of the football team, but the younger Gabriel is mysteriously *good* and Christ-like.) Another world. There were the thrilling adventures of Judy Bolton, Girl Detective. But my favorite book, one that I checked out obsessively, was *The Winged Girl of Knossos.* The (metaphorically) winged girl is training to be a "bull-dancer" in ancient Crete. She practices and practices and eventually learns to perform the near-impossible feat of three somersaults over the bull's back during the sacred rituals. The book contained color illustrations based on ancient Minoan wall frescoes. How I loved that story! I had to surface from each reading like a diver floating slowly up from the deep, very slowly, so as not to get the bends.

The school at 637 Madison Avenue accepted me but placed me in "A" class with the beginners. Forget everything you've been taught and start right. At first I took lessons three times a week, but doubled that when I was promoted to "B" (Intermediate) class and was allowed to ride the BMT to 59th Street and back all by myself. By the time I was in "C" (Advanced) I was taking the nine lessons a week expected of a serious ballet student.

We studied with gentle, balding Pierre Vladimiroff, who was said to have been Anna Pavlova's favorite partner and who took on Nijinsky's roles when that phenomenon left the Imperial Russian Ballet for good. Vladimiroff wore soft-soled leather shoes and I never heard him make a sound as he moved about the room or showed us steps. The barre exercises and floor work in his classes were accompanied by the delicate, tinkling strains of Chopin, Glinka, Delibes, and Tchaikovsky. He preferred the Romantics and would abide no barbaric musical newcomers. A few years later, Mr. Balanchine persuaded Vlady's wife, the inimitable Felia Doubrovska, to teach our professional class. This modest, elegant woman had danced the roles of Polyhymnia, then Terpsichore, in Balanchine's breakthrough success, *Apollon Musagète*, and the role of the Seductress in *The Prodigal Son*. In her sixties, she still possessed a willowy figure. Doubrovska, though tall, was ethereal in manner. She never walked on the ground. She floated.

Anatole Oboukhov was our dread but beloved taskmaster. He was gaunt, angular, and short, and he terrified us. Not long after he'd joined the faculty of the School, he was instructed not to use a cane in class to correct the students; parents had lodged a complaint. (He snorted, they say, but left the cane home.) Mr. Oboukhov dressed in long-sleeved starched white shirts, dark blue trousers, and periodically whipped out an immaculate white handkerchief and loudly blew his nose. His hair was slicked close to a narrow skull, and his gaze was penetrating. He would survey us grimly as we stood at the barre, pulled up tight but quaking inside; then after a few long moments during which nobody dared breathe, he would deliver a shrill, ascending "e-e-e-e-e" ("a-a-a-a-n-d"), signaling the pianist, and us, to begin. Or, as he pronounced it: "Begin-yin!" He smelled faintly of lavender water and the strong breath mints he used—it was murmured—to cover the whiff of alcohol. His classes were the most difficult. If you missed a step, or failed to balance, or fell off a pirouette, or came down too hard from a jump, you'd hear a scornful "Ha!! Oho!!" Of course he was the one who gave us the stamina we needed for performances. And he sometimes had a twinkle in his dark Russian eye.

There was English Muriel Stuart who had danced with Pavlova's company. She taught class in sleeveless floating chiffon outfits and acrobatic sandals, and was forever reminding us with clipped articulation to "tuck in the place you sit upon!" Along with our daily lesson in soft ballet shoes, we took Pointe Class, in toe shoes; Modern in sandals; Adagio, on pointe with a partner; Variations, learning solo parts from the classical repertoire; and Character (national dances), in shiny black patent-leather shoes with low heels for stamping. Yura Lazowsky, another hard taskmaster—but handsome!—taught Character Class: the wild Czardas, the elegant Mazurka, the Spanish Hat Dance, the Polonaise.

We taught each other as well. Stayed after class and practiced turns and balances and runs and beats and jumps. Critiqued and corrected and competed with each other, suggested ways to do better. We made friends and sneaked into the ballet together. We became "supers" (extra bodies) on stage at the Met and the City Center. We read *Dance Magazine* and subscribed to Lincoln Kirstein's *Dance Index*. We lived and breathed and talked Dance. We worked hard, set high goals, drove ourselves, and improved. We grew impatient to move into "D" class and become professionals.

Intended or not, I was on my way to becoming a dancer. I was going to perform in cities all over Europe and across America. I was going to dance before crowned heads, and be part of the first group of American dancers ever to perform at the White House. I was going to become a soloist in Balanchine's company. I was going to see the world.

Symphonie Concertante (1949). *Far left:* Pat McBride; *Left column (front to back):* Margaret Walker, Ruth Sobotka, Charlotte Ray (?), Una Kai; *Right column (front to back):* Peggy Karlson, Doris Breckenridge, Barbara Milberg (looking the wrong way), Arlouine Case. Photo by Fred Fehl, copyright G. Pinksi, author's collection.

I

Balanchine's Company

My FIRST PERFORMANCE was with Ballet Society in Mozart's *Symphonie Concertante*: corps de ballet, eighteenth-century music, simple steps, white *tutu*. Within a year of that performance in November 1947, Balanchine's small experimental group would officially become the New York City Ballet. My last ballet with the company was *Agon*, premiered in 1957: soloist, Stravinsky score, complex movements, black leotard. These two ballets, spaced ten years apart, project a range from the classical to the postmodern. Both were staged at the City Center of Music and Drama in New York and both were choreographed by George Balanchine.

Before I left the company in 1958, the year after I married, to join Jerry Robbins's newly formed Ballets: USA as a principle dancer, I traveled with the New York City Ballet on five European tours and three coast-to-coast American tours. The company's first venture overseas was during the summer of 1950. We danced to packed houses at Covent Garden Opera House, at that time the home of the Saddlers Wells Ballet, in a London still devastated from the bombings of World War II. England was in the grip of austerity, and we were issued ration coupons for meat, eggs, sugar, and soap. During the 1950s we performed in two other theaters, beside Covent Garden, that no longer exist. By the close of the century both the Gran Liceo, in Barcelona, and the centuries-old Teatro La Fenice, in Venice, had burned to the ground.

Our overseas tours generally lasted from two to five months. Back home, regular seasons in New York alternated with shorter seasons in Chicago and we danced in Baltimore, Philadelphia, and Washington on stages never meant for ballet. On the West Coast we performed at the Greek Theater in Los Angeles on an open-air stage—open also to large winged insects attracted to sweating bodies—and the company returned several times to San Francisco's War Memorial Opera House where a rare dance audience received us warmly. We danced in Red Rocks, Colorado, at such an altitude you could scarcely breathe, with an oxygen tank stationed just off the stage-right wing. The opening ballet that night was Tchaikovsky's *Serenade* and I was one of the four girls in the "Little Russian Dance," which required running and jumping and frenzied sprinting behind the backdrop to enter from the opposite side of the stage on time. Except at Red Rocks there was no backdrop. To accomplish the crossover, we four scrambled down concrete steps, dashed along a narrow passageway below stage-level, up another set of steps, and emerged on the other side only to fly across the stage and disappear with exploding lungs into the wings. The one time I made for the oxygen tank, wheezing and gasping for air, Casey (Arlouine Case), who'd run offstage moments before, reeled and fainted right in front of me and they clamped the mask on her.

In the summer of 1956, Balanchine set dances to the music of his beloved Mozart and we performed these chamber pieces at the Shakespeare Theatre in Stratford, Connecticut, in celebration of the composer's bicentennial. On the continent we danced before crowned heads in the great opera houses of London, the Netherlands and Monaco; we performed at the Opera and the Théâtre de Champs Élysées in Paris, at La Scala in Milan. In Venice we danced at La Fenice, that gilded little jewel-box of a theater that burned down in the 1990s. We danced before fascists in Barcelona and Lisbon. In Trieste there was terror in the streets and a virtually empty opera house; a military coup d'etat was in progress and armed soldiers with cartridge belts patrolled the city. In Rome the Opera Guild had a medal struck for us and every dancer received one—gold, silver, bronze for the corps. I still have mine.

We danced under conditions never envisioned by the American Guild of Musical Artists, our union. If our consignment of pointe shoes did not arrive, we danced in shoes temporarily stiffened by spirit gum—the strong glue actors use to attach hair pieces and moustaches—and sometimes in shoes so worn that the only protection between the stage and our toes was layers of heavy brown paper. We danced on blisters. We danced when we felt ill; we danced with "stone bruises"; we danced on sprained ankles tightly bandaged with strips of one-inch adhesive tape. We performed on "raked" stages tilted sharply downwards toward the audience, careful to avoid slightly sunken trapdoors. We danced on ancient wood floors thick with splinters, on floors thinly laid over concrete. We jumped in when someone had an accident. We learned how to massage sore necks and shoulders and aching cramped calloused feet. We learned how to ask for "backstage" and "the check, please" in French, Spanish, German, Italian, Dutch, Danish, and Portuguese and we all grew proficient in currency exchange.

En route to the next city or country we wrote home, read magazines, novels, and murder mysteries, did crossword puzzles, napped, gossiped, or simply stared out the train windows. Some took this time to darn the tips of their pointe shoes and sew on pink satin ribbons. A few hard-core addicts played serious poker, hands dealt out on a not-too-level suitcase supported by four or five sets of knees. No wild cards.

As a touring company, we rehearsed together, roomed together, ate together, traveled together. Never again would I feel such a charged, all-engulfing sense of purpose; we were determined to achieve recognition against enormous odds. And while there were the inevitable complaints, clashes, petty rebellions, snits and grumps—plus the occasional temperamental explosion—this sense of purpose bound us together from the newest, greenest member of the corps to the directors of the company. Everybody worked unbelievably long hours, not only Balanchine, Lincoln Kirstein, and our executive manager Betty Cage, but also rehearsal pianists, stage directors, wardrobe keepers, and, when necessary, the entire staff at Madame Barbara Karinska's costuming establishment.

During all the years I danced with the company—save one, the year after Balanchine's fourth wife, Tanaquil Le Clercq, contracted polio—Mr. Balanchine was there with us, a kind of polymorphous presence. He was the teacher who gave company class, the primary choreographer who rehearsed us at home and on tour. He traveled with us on plane, train, and boat. He attended the parties. He was at Karinska's, superintending costume fittings; he was in the house at lighting rehearsals conferring with Jean Rosenthal, our owlish inventive lighting director. He was present during orchestra rehearsals of new ballets. He stood in the wings during the performance. Sometimes it seemed as if the company were flowing out of his veins.

With Lincoln, who was constantly on the lookout for philanthropic "angels," and Betty Cage who was something of a quiet genius in management, Balanchine made sure we danced at the best theaters, had decent living accommodations. We almost never did one-night stands. At a period when funding was always uncertain and sometimes nil, we flew over the Atlantic first class in a BOAC Stratocruiser that boasted a downstairs lounge and carried the entire company, the staff, a rehearsal pianist, our conductor, and key members of the orchestra. Travel and rehearsal schedules were posted, wages paid on time. Everything but dancing was taken care of.

Balanchine trained us the way a gardener will espalier a tree to gain the most sunlight. He realigned our limbs, pruned and replaced, crossbred and experimented, demonstrated and patiently corrected, scolded, teased—and occasionally made fun of us. His ridicule could be devastating. I remember one difficult class when he set out to improve his prize pupil's *entrechat-six*, a vertical jump in which the legs beat back and forth and back again on the way down. Nicely done, with legs turned out, feet pointed down and knees very straight, the beats are crisp and distinct. "Tanny," he drawled to his long-legged future ballerina and wife, "your legs look like asparagus—*cooked* asparagus!"

On the other hand, Balanchine's gift for imagery could be genuinely helpful. "Reach for gold!" he whispered loudly to a dancer who was wobbling on one leg in a long-held *arabesque penchée*, he dangling the imaginary treasure just out of reach of her outstretched arm. The wobbling stopped. Another's shaky arabesque was steadied with "ice-cream, *delicious* ice-cream." Balanchine knew who to tempt with what. "Come down on *eggs!*" he directed a boy who was landing too heavily from a jump. It transformed the whole dynamics of the movement. Later, he would take the time to coach him, demonstrate to all of us how "like a *cat*" you land first on the ball of the foot, then slowly roll down to the heel. Sometimes, crouching down with two strong hands clamped around your foot and ankle, he would do it for you, with you, make sure you got the feel of it.

He was the husbandman for whom the least detail was significant, every element worthy of attention. This slender Georgian émigré with his limitless drive and laser focus was more than our major choreographer, more than our director, more than our teacher and goad. He was very simply the constant in the equation, our company's shaping spirit.

Milberg at Bethesda Fountain in Central Park, New York City
(spring 1951). Photo, Ernst Beadle, author's collection.

2

Schools

ℳHEN MR. BALANCHINE asked me to join Ballet Society in the fall of 1946, I was not quite fifteen and had to have my parents' consent to perform on stage. Balanchine was preparing for the oncoming season at the City Center of Music and Drama, and strains of Mozart leaked out each time young dancers in practice clothes slipped into one of the larger studios. Some of my classmates at the School of American Ballet were already in rehearsal. How I longed to be one of the chosen, hurrying from the dressing room to the studio, trailing a towel to mop up the sweat. I watched them enter the room, easing the heavy soundproof door open and closing it behind as quietly as possible. As it happens, I was in luck. One of the girls in the corps had dropped out, gone home somewhere in the Midwest, and Mr. B needed a replacement.

He walked into my evening "C" class that day in the khaki pants and striped navy and white polo shirt he wore for rehearsals, nodded courteously to Pierre Vladimiroff who was conducting the class, and sat down on the low bench that spanned the wall of mirrors. A kind of electric current passed through the room. He'd never come to look at us before.

Our soft-spoken "Vlady" was something of a legend in himself. In Russia, he'd taken over Vaslav Nijinsky's roles and he was reputed to have been Pavlova's favorite partner. Balanchine, attentive and inscrutable, watched as Vladimiroff divided us into two groups. He watched us go through the agonizingly slow "adagio" steps, then jump and turn and skim over the floor in quick allegro combinations. I knew I was better at fast pirouettes and soaring jumps then at sustained adagio work, and like everyone else in that class I felt charged with energy and excitement. Each time the second group was on the floor dancing "full out," I leaned against the barre that ran around three walls of the studio, panting and wiping the sweat from my face and eyes.

At the end of class, as always, we did a formal "*réverence*" to measured legato chords, bowing deeply to our teacher. When I came up drenched in sweat and breathing hard, Omigod! Mr. Balanchine was right in front of me. I could see those Georgian cheekbones, the carved eagle nose, intent dark eyes. "Barbara" he said, pronouncing all three syllables of my name with his slightly nasal intonation, "will you like to be in my *Symphonia Concertante?*" I could feel my heart pounding, my face grow more flushed than before. I was able to croak one word—yes! He nodded, looked pleased, and told me to ask the secretary when rehearsal would be tomorrow. And to get my parents' permission. Then he bowed slightly to Vlady and left the room. It wasn't until late that night, nearly asleep, as I played the scene over and over and over, that I realized he'd called me "Barbara." How did Mr. Balanchine know my name?

Then I remembered. The G Minor sonata, the shadowy room. How could I have forgotten? But he hadn't asked my name. . . .

I'm at the piano in an empty studio, working on the Schubert G Minor sonata. I've just been accepted into the highly competitive High School of Music and Art, and at the same time been promoted from "B" (Intermediate) to "C" (Advanced) class at the School of American Ballet. Weekdays, I hop on the double-decker bus at 135th Street and St. Nicholas Avenue and head down a two-way Fifth Avenue to the School at Madison and 59th Street for my ballet class, sometimes two classes in one day. Every Saturday I ride the subway from Flatbush to my ballet lesson. If the big studio is empty, I can practice after class on the Mason and Hamlin grand piano, with its rich resonant bass and clear treble. And this instrument is tuned regularly, unlike the baby grand with the cracked soundboard at home.

This particular afternoon I've been attacking the Schubert, still in my practice clothes. Nobody's around to inhibit me and there's no reason to restrain the volume as the doors to all three studios are soundproof. I'd gone over the opening measures until I was satisfied and now I'm beginning to play "with feeling," as they used to say, increasingly carried away by the passion of the music. Sometimes I strike a wrong note and stop to run over the passage a couple of times. The overhead lights are not switched on and the room has grown darkish, but I'm playing from memory so it doesn't really matter so long as I can see the keyboard.

I don't hear the door open, or notice the figure that has moved quietly toward the piano until he's almost at my shoulder. Then I stop dead. I recognize Mr. Balanchine. The head of the School of American Ballet. Balanchine, who choreographed *Night Shadow* and *Ballet Imperial*; who had set the unbelievably beautiful *Concerto Barocco* to the Bach D Minor double violin concerto. He must have been changing in the male teachers' dressing room, located in the dark little passage between the reception area and the large studio—and heard the Schubert.

"Go on" he says, very gently. I shake my head.

"Please, go on, play some more," he urges. I shake my head again, look down at the keyboard.

"I can't." I'm too shy, unprepared for the intrusion, overwhelmed by the man's presence. I look up after a bit and mumble "I'm sorry." I really am.

"That's all right," he says kindly, smiles, nods, and withdraws.

Balanchine and Kirstein had formed Ballet Society as an experimental enterprise, a kind of research lab for the arts, not for profit but to develop new ideas. Principal dancers like Marie-Jeanne, William Dollar, and Lew Christensen were drawn from their original small touring companies, the American Ballet and Ballet Caravan. Sinuous, intelligent Todd Bolender, gifted dancer and choreographer, had done his apprenticeship with Hanya Holm, who headed a well-known modern dance ensemble; while sabre-legged Mary Ellen Moylan, the high-flying Patricia Wilde and, a bit later, the exquisitely musical Maria Tallchief (who would soon become Balanchine's third wife and the company's prima ballerina) had all danced principal roles with Serge Denham's company, the Ballet Russe de Monte Carlo. Mr. B selected students from the School of American Ballet for his corps de ballet dancers and used the school's three studios for rehearsal space. Four times a year, Ballet Society presented contemporary works to a sophisticated audience on a subscription basis. Most often a work was brand new, although the Society occasionally staged a radical experiment in sound or form that had been conceived and produced in Europe but never shown in the United States.

Performances usually took place in cramped high school and college auditoriums and once, as I recall, rather more grandly at the old Ziegfeld Theater on Sixth Avenue. Two years before, in 1945, I had watched the original presentation of the Mozart *Symphony Concertante* at Carnegie Hall, along with two shorter works set to Stravinsky music. Carnegie Hall had irreproachable acoustics and the house was more chastely appointed than the Ziegfeld, but the stage was specifically designed to accommodate concert artists. It was not deep enough for ballet and the dancers had to be thinned out. At that time, only two theaters in the city could sustain a full classical ballet: the old Metropolitan Opera House, the great "Golden Horseshoe" with its red velvet boxes and gold brocaded curtain, located in the midst of the garment district in the West 30s; and the City Center of Music and Drama, a converted Masonic

Temple. We heard, however, from dancers who had been on tour that the rest of the country was an aesthetic desert. A wasteland. Even the nation's capital had no opera house, only Constitution Hall which was designed, like Carnegie Hall, for individual concert artists, chamber groups, and lectures.

In the 1940s, New Yorkers could attend Grand Opera and symphony concerts in season. They could go to plays on Broadway or hit the Cotton Club in Harlem for some cool jazz; or they might take in a "bread and butter" program of *Swan Lake*, *Nutcracker*, *Scheherazade*, when Denham's Ballet Russe arrived in town. The rival company, American Ballet Theatre, alternated *Giselle* and a full-length *Sleeping Beauty*, the classic "old warhorses," with a tastefully elegiac *Lilac Garden* by the English choreographer Antony Tudor, or a forthright piece of Americana such as *Fall River Legend*, or later, *Rodeo*. *Rodeo*, with a score by the American composer Aaron Copland, was premiered originally by Denham's Ballet Russe in 1942 and swiftly followed by the Broadway musical *Oklahoma!* in 1943. Both reflected the nation's love affair with "Westerns" and both the ballet and the musical were choreographed by Agnes de Mille. Her *Fall River Legend* was another story. It attempted a Freudian study of Lizzie Borden, a real-life New England murderess who, according to the folk ballad, "took an ax / And gave her mother forty whacks, / And when she saw what she had done / Gave her father forty-one." American themes were patriotic in the forties. By 1944, Ballet Theatre had staged young Jerry Robbins's *Fancy Free*—a jazzy ballet about three American sailors on leave in wartime New York—a wildly popular "hit" that right away morphed into the Broadway show, *On the Town*. American as Ginger Rogers and Fred Astaire.

But four times a year, for a week or two, you could see a brilliant or bizarre new ballet, or a surreal opera, with sets and costumes designed by a contemporary artist. Tchelitchew, perhaps, or Kurt Seligmann or Joan Junyer or Cecil Beaton. You could hear scores composed by Stravinsky, Hindemith, Rieti, Barber, Ravel. Or you might be treated to a pure classical abstraction, danced on pointe in white *tutus* and pink silk tights, not to the romantic strains of

Premiere of Robbins's *The Guests* (1948). In foreground: Maria Tallchief, Jerome Robbins, composer Marc Blitzstein; Milberg at center back. Photo by Fred Fehl, copyright, G. Pinski, author's collection.

Tchaikovsky or Chopin, but to Mozart. And while not every performance ushered in a masterpiece—indeed there were flops—there was a sense of daring, an authentic overarching vision. Ballet Society's offerings were bold, imaginative, controversial. Unlike any other theater-arts project in the country, Ballet Society brought the Modernist explosion home. It was the seedcase out of which sprang, in 1948, the New York City Ballet.

3

Introducing Stravinsky

ORKING WITH BALANCHINE was a good way to spoil you. In rehearsal, he had a quiet manner and the concentration of a cabinet maker putting together a complicated piece of furniture. He knew what he wanted and could let you know in the simplest terms, either by verbal direction or, more often, by demonstrating. He was comfortably impersonal when he was working, yet at the same time keenly attentive. Balanchine possessed a kind of multidimensional alertness that included the immediate phrase of music and the spatial design of the sequence he was envisioning, but also an uncanny awareness of the physical idiom of the dancer he was working with, the way that person naturally moved. As Maria Tallchief observed many years later, "He never pushed a dancer or raised his voice. He never bullied. . . . He was patient. He let a dancer in on the process, allowed her to see what was happening." Maria notes the "moral dimension," the discipline informing Balanchine's interaction with his dancers: "There were no shortcuts, no easy tricks, just a pure and simple approach."[1]

You watched closely while he thought through a series of movements in his own body. The steps might be syncopated or, if he was working with a group, the timing contrapuntal. Sometimes he'd take a dancer by the hand or just above the elbow or, more abstractedly, by the wrist, and so connected begin to work out a complex series of movements. Or, intent on some interior design, his head bent down, he might slowly walk you to another position in the room, moving as if through water instead of air. You felt like a chess piece, placed with deliberation. Often the only sound in the studio was a repeated phrase of music or a murmured instruction to the pianist, in Russian: "*Mozhno*, Kolya." Go ahead.

People who accused him of genius were set straight immediately: "I am not genius, I am craftsman." If they waxed enthusiastic about his "creative" abilities, Balanchine gravely corrected them: "Only God creates; I assemble." Of course he was a genius and a fountain of invention. But he may have felt that ego-swelling would dry up the cascade of ideas, deprive him of grace. Those closest to him knew that Balanchine possessed an almost childlike religious belief; and we were all aware of his observance of Russian Orthodox rituals. We knew he prepared the elaborate Russian Easter feast each year with his own hands, cooking and baking for days in advance, dashing at times between home and rehearsal. Surely, his great affection for Stravinsky was nurtured by their common background, not only in their memories of the Russian homeland, or the shared mother tongue, but in observance of the rites that expressed their origins.

While Mr. B could be playful, even mischievous, he possessed a sharp sardonic streak. He was capable of a brutal directness, as when he parodied one dancer (a bit too perfectly) collapsing after a high jump into "sack of potatoes," or told another that although she might dance the Swan Queen one day, *he* would not go to see it. Yet one was reminded time and again of the man's innate courtesy. When he was working with children his manner was serious, tactful, firm; you sensed a mutual respect flowing between the young dancers and their choreographer. But you also might see a grave or intently focused Balanchine suddenly turn playful.

He displayed this most engaging aspect of his personality one afternoon, early in the spring of 1948, when Igor Stravinsky arrived at the School on Madison Avenue to observe a rehearsal of "Furies" in *Orpheus*.

Stravinsky had been commissioned to write the music for the ballet. The premiere was scheduled for late April that year, and the composer himself would be conducting on opening night. Balanchine's first collaboration with Stravinsky in 1928 had put the younger man on the map. In *Apollon Musagète* ("Apollo and the Muses"), the twenty-four-year-old choreographer had breathtakingly combined classical ballet and classical Greek images with modern jazz. Balanchine later described the collaboration and the resulting choreographic breakthrough as "the turning point in my life." First performed in Paris, on June 12, by the Russian-trained dancers of Serge Diaghilev's Ballets Russes, *Apollon Musagète* was soon recognized as a turning point in the history of dance: It changed irrevocably the perception of what was possible in ballet.

Now, some twenty years later, Balanchine and Stravinsky once again were collaborating on the recreation of an ancient Greek myth; this time, the myth of a divinely gifted musician. Balanchine on the East Coast and Stravinsky in California had arranged meetings. According to Bernard Taper, Balanchine's biographer, they'd been conferring, plotting it out, piecing it together between June 1946 and the fall of 1947 when Stravinsky completed the score.[2] Together, they had been able to unloose the mystery, the beauty, the drama, and the violence inherent in a primitive religious ritual. Balanchine worked tirelessly as the date appointed for the premiere approached, and our usually self-contained Mr. B seemed eager, full of energy, as he began to set actual movements for the actual dancers.

As always, he choreographed each section separately. First he set the principal parts: Nicholas Magellanes as Orpheus, the poet-singer whose lyre moves trees and wild animals; Maria Tallchief as Eurydice, his bride, bitten by a poisonous snake on their wedding day; and the noble, bronze-complexioned Francisco Moncion, cast as the Dark Angel, the Hermes-like *psychopompos* or "conductor of

Orpheus (1948). Francisco Moncion as the Dark Angel, Nicholas Magallanes as Orpheus, Maria Tallchief as Eurydice; Beatrice Tompkins, Chief Fury, kneeling right foreground. Photograph by Fred Fehl with permission of Gabriel Pinski, www.FredFehl.com. Jerome Robbins Dance Division, The New York Public Library for the Performing Arts, Astor, Lenox and Tilden Foundations.

souls," who guides Orpheus to Hades to plead for the return of his beloved. Hermes, in Greek myth, is the messenger god who can move freely between celestial, earthly, and underworld realms, and is thus well appointed to conduct the dead to the land of shades. But Frank's Dark Angel also had something of Dante's figure of Virgil in the *Inferno*, the companion and mentor who guides the living poet into the depths of Hell.

Balanchine had devised the most extraordinarily moving passage for the two men, in which the Dark Angel leads the grief-stricken poet ever deeper into the realm of the dead, his lyre hanging upon their linked arms, or thrown back and forth over half the stage in constant play between them. Orpheus's lyre, his irresistible music, enchants Pluto, lord of the underworld, and effects Eurydice's re-

Maria Tallchief as Eurydice in *Orpheus* (1948). Photo: George Platt Lynes, © Estate of George Platt Lynes. Jerome Robbins Dance Division, The New York Public Library for the Performing Arts, Astor, Lenox and Tilden Foundations.

lease. Balanchine had already choreographed the *pas de deux*, expertly handling its challenge: Nicky must dance with Maria without ever looking at her—until the unbearable moment when, just as a glimmer of light appears from the upper world, he glances back—and she disappears. Taper perfectly captured both the intricacy and the agony of that *pas de deux*, "in which she twines herself about him beseechingly while he desperately tries to carry out the injunction that he not look at her . . . a tour de force," he writes, "yet so loving, so poignant, so infused with erotic urgency that the spectator would be scarcely aware of its choreographic virtuosity."[3] After these sections, Mr. B put together the violently syncopated, stabbing movements of the Bacchantes, the female devotees of Dionysos, who tear the doubly bereft Orpheus limb from limb. Their leader was the long-legged angular Tanaquil Le Clercq, whose dramatic flair leaped to the forefront in this role.

At the time of Stravinsky's visit, Balanchine was sketching out "Furies," the section I was in, though happily promoted to "Bacchantes" shortly before I received demi-soloist billing. "Furies" was probably the last section on the rehearsal agenda, save for the final elegiac solo, the swelling "Apotheosis" made for Herbert Bliss as the sun-god Apollo, the beautiful Immortal, the god of proportion and music—a transcendent allusion, perhaps, to the origins of the Balanchine/Stravinsky partnership. Pretty soon Mr. B would put all the parts together as a chef might assemble ingredients, and we dancers would see the whole of *Orpheus* from beginning to end, the very first viewing it would have.

Balanchine behaved toward Stravinsky the way most of us behaved toward Balanchine, with a respect verging on reverence. They were attuned, we felt, in some mysterious private way. After seeing them together over the years, however briefly, we came to expect that when the composer appeared in the rehearsal room, he and Balanchine would plunge into Russian, argue, gesticulate, disagree, huddle with the pianist and generally give the impression that they were enjoying themselves immensely. Perhaps on this particular day, the day we first met him, the spirit of mischief arrived with the composer.

When not actually dancing my part in "Furies," I'd been page-turning for Nicholas Kopeikine, Balanchine's rehearsal pianist and lifelong colleague. "Kolya" had been a child prodigy, and was a young concert pianist at the time of the Russian Revolution. He was the son of a prominent businessman whose wealth, it seems, derived from the production of brass buttons for all the military uniforms in the Tsar's army. Once Kolya told us how, deciding impulsively not to return to a Russia suddenly become Communist and dangerous, he had jumped off a train in Poland—jumped from his family's private railroad car as the train slowed down—and run across fields of snow with the family jewels sewn into the lining of his sable coat. He made his way to Monte Carlo, which is probably where Kopeikine and Balanchine met, and the young defector earned his living for a time playing in brothels and in movie theaters for silent films.

Now, some thirty years hence, it was hard to envision Kolya as a young fugitive. He was an imposing figure, large, leonine, and very portly, all the way to the tips of pudgy fingers, and his chins wobbled when he played *fortissimo*. He dressed with care. His mane of white hair had a faint tint of blue, and for such a large man his voice was surprisingly high, ranging at times to falsetto. We played chess once or twice in the reception area, waiting for a class to let out of a rehearsal room, and Kolya easily won—although he reported to Mr. Balanchine that I was "not so bad." He was an accomplished and versatile pianist, and I felt honored when he allowed me to turn pages for him.

The music for "Furies" was an orchestra score, newly delivered, that Kopeikine was transposing to piano at a first reading with virtually no mistakes. I admired Stravinsky's beautiful spidery manuscript notation and was thrilled to learn that the celebrated composer was expected at rehearsal within the hour. When Stravinsky finally appeared, however, I was more astonished than anything else. He came up to Mr. B's shoulder in height and resembled a bright-eyed cartoon mouse in his raincoat and homburg hat. We stared at him, trying to look as though we were not staring. He looked inquiringly at us.

The Furies were not cast as Eumenides, the terrible triumvirate of classical tragedy who pursue the hero without mercy in Aeschylus's *Oresteia*. We were not those "Proud Furies, each with her torch on high" as the Irish poet, William Butler Yeats, envisioned them. The Furies in *Orpheus* were nameless denizens of Hades, proletarian demons, whose job was to torment certain poor souls

Cut-outs of costumes for *Orpheus* by designer Isamu Noguchi. © 2005 The Isamu Noguchi Foundation and Garden Museum, New York / Artists Rights Society (ARS) New York, and Jerome Robbins Dance Division, The New York Public Library for the Performing Arts, Astor, Lenox and Tilden Foundations.

doomed to carry massive rocks through eternity. Isamu Noguchi had designed nasty gray body-suits for us with tentacles springing out all over, some from really embarrassing places. We were colorless, third-class, corps-de-ballet monsters. Orpheus would come by at the close of our threatening dance, pluck music from his lyre, and give the rock-bearers a temporary break.

You had to wonder. Why did Balanchine and Stravinsky depart so radically from earlier representations? Why had they chosen such a grim, colorless character for their tormentors? Were we, perhaps, Stalinist Furies? Ghosts from the realm these two Russians had fled? Memory traces of Soviet *apparatchiks*, petty bureaucrats with just enough political power to burden ordinary lives beyond bearing? When the composer entered the studio, Mr. B stopped the rehearsal and greeted his friend with warmth. He saw us staring at Stravinsky and Stravinsky taking us in. He must have decided on the spot to personally introduce all nine Furies, each one separately, to the composer. "Come!" he said to the mouse apparition, "I want you to meet Furies." Kolya's hands dropped from the keys onto his lap. Stravinsky removed his hat, a gallant gesture.

Balanchine led him in a great circle around the rehearsal room and, stopping before each of us, intoned "Mister Stravinsky . . . Miss Few-ry," "Mister Stravinsky . . . Miss Few-ry," "Mister Stravinsky . . . Miss Few-ry," until eight little monsters and one Chief Fury, Beatrice Tompkins, had been formally introduced. At each presentation Stravinsky drew his heels together smartly and bowed with military precision. I felt as though I'd been received at Court. Mr. B looked very pleased with his little composer and his little joke; it had broken the ice and put everyone at ease. Stravinsky was invited to the bench in front of the mirror, we were signaled to take our places, and Balanchine inclined his head toward the piano: *Mozhno, Kolya!*

Orpheus, with its billowing curtain of white parachute silk, its spare Noguchi sets and costumes, its magical lighting, its violent climax and noble Apotheosis, reenacted tragic drama in its most ancient ritual form—dance. It was potent theatre. On opening night the action unfolded with a kind of inevitability, gaining in momentum from the instant of the protagonist's disastrous glance backward and the disappearance of his beloved, sucked into and swallowed by billowing clouds of parachute silk. Then the swift change of pace, the plucked aggressive chords, the startling shift from semi-darkness to brilliant light. In this severe brilliance, this light suggesting the uncompromising clarity of an operating room, the Bacchantes dismember the poet, his arms torn off one after the other, both legs, the head. Finally the Apotheosis, the slow turning motions of the Sun God, lighting all things with the great gold

Herbert Bliss as the god Apollo in *Orpheus*, performing the poignant "Apotheosis" in the closing scene of the ballet. Photo George Platt Lynes, © Estate of George Platt Lynes. Jerome Robbins Dance Division, The New York Public Library for the Performing Arts, Astor, Lenox and Tilden Foundations.

mask of the sun. At the very last, the lyre that marks the grave of Orpheus is elevated, lifted high above the stage on invisible cable, a floating emblem.

It left the audience shaken. A period of stark silence followed the closing notes of harp and horn, the descent of the final curtain, while people recovered themselves and found their hands and voices. That night it seemed the applause and shouts and bouquets would never stop, for Balanchine, for Stravinsky, for Noguchi, for the lighting director, for the principal dancers, for us. I think we sensed right away that *Orpheus* had done more for our struggling young company than simply overwhelm the opening night audience and impress the dance critics. That spring season of 1948 marked the point when the New York City Ballet began to be counted as one of the city's major theatrical attractions. We had arrived.

4

Politics

ONE AFTERNOON early in October 1948, I scooted up the steps to the stage entrance of the City Center on West 56th Street, said "hi" to the guard stationed at the door, and headed backstage for rehearsal with a large blue-and-white "VOTE FOR WALLACE" button pinned to the lapel of my coat. At this point, the Company was about to be designated New York City's official ballet troupe, I was completing my senior year at high school, and a presidential election was coming up in November. For most Americans, the November election meant a battle between Harry S. Truman, the Democratic incumbent, and Governor Thomas E. Dewey, the conservative Republican challenger. My family, which leaned to the left about as far as you can lean without falling over, supported the Progressive Party candidate.

Mr. Balanchine must have spotted my campaign button as soon as I walked in. He came up behind me as I stood scanning the rehearsal schedule at the bulletin board and, to my astonishment, asked me to remove it. "Barbara, take off bahton, *please!*" he said with some urgency. "Don't wear that." I refused, outraged. What had my politics to do with my work? I stood there facing him without uttering a word, making no move to comply. My heart began to beat faster and I felt a blush heating my cheeks. I was indignant—but also scared. Was Mr. B going to fire me for wearing a third-party campaign button?

Henry Wallace was considered a "pinko." He'd been Franklin Delano Roosevelt's Secretary of Agriculture and then his Vice-President until 1946. At that point, as novelist Philip Roth noted many years later in a story for *The New Yorker*, the President "fired Wallace for sounding off in favor of coöperation with Stalin and the Soviet Union."[1]

My mother and father had both grown up in rural *shtetls* (Jewish enclaves, ghettos) just outside Odessa in the Ukraine. They had emigrated from a Tsarist Russia, my mother with her family, my father on his own, and they knew something about oppression. Both had arrived in this country via "steerage," crowded with other impoverished travelers for weeks in the belly of a ship. Both had struggled with a new language, worked unbelievable hours as non-union labor, gone to night school, become citizens, and made their way against tremendous odds into the professional class. They had met and married in this country, lived through two World Wars (my father a veteran of the First) and survived the Great Depression. They belonged to a generation for whom "politics" meant—not spin-doctoring—but the struggle between opposed philosophies of government. For my parents, the newly formed Progressive Party emitted a rosy Socialist glow. It represented a political ideal of universal entitlement, the chance to "make something of yourself" no matter how humble your origins.

Mr. Balanchine also knew something about oppression. He had escaped, not a Tsarist, but a Soviet straitjacket. For him, the utopian society already existed, right here in America. So when I arrived for rehearsal sporting a conspicuous "VOTE FOR WALLACE" button and stubbornly refused to remove it, he took firm hold of my elbow and walked me to a quiet corner. I guess he had me pegged as an uninformed young idealist. In truth, I was unaware of the privations he had undergone, ignorant of the rigid conditions imposed by the Soviet state. As he saw it, I was making a terrible mistake. "You don't understand," he said, and I could see he was searching for the right words. "Communist country is *lousy* place! Can't say what you want. People spy, talk behind back. Friend disappear. Nobody free. Everybody hungry, all the time hungry. Here is good," he went on, patting my shoulder. "Best place. Do what you want. Say what you like, vote how you like. Wonderful country, not like Communist." It went something like that. Finally, he spoke of the difficulty he and his little band of dancers experienced trying to leave Soviet Russia: "Almost, they didn't let us go!" He let me go then. I think he knew I'd paid attention to what he was telling me, that I understood there was another side to be considered. Out of principle however, or sheer obstinacy, or maybe simple logic, I continued to wear the Wallace button. After all, Mr. B was celebrating the freedom to "vote how you like"—and he didn't seem disposed to fire me.

Not too long after this encounter I notice a gaggle of dancers gathered around someone during a break, bursting into peals of laughter. What's going on? I squeeze in and find Mr. B at the center sitting on a theater trunk, transformed into a fat, self-important *apparatchik*. This troll is installed (by way of pantomime) behind a mountain of papers at an imaginary desk. Our choreographer now performs a wicked parody of the petty customs official who detained and tormented the little group of dancers about to leave Russia with hard-won permission, supposedly for a brief concert tour but planning never to return. This was that desperate moment, I realized, of *Almost, they didn't let us go!* A consummate mime, Balanchine metamorphosed into his younger self, became various anxiety-ridden dancers, male and female, who were trying to appear unconcerned. Then he turned once more into the sadistic official who repeatedly delayed their embarkation; showed us how this man had kept them waiting as he pretended to study their papers; how he'd finally passed them through the checkpoint; how he'd recall one, then another, with a beckoning arm as though he'd just discovered some incriminating flaw, some defect that invalidated the papers; then demanded more documents, more proof of official permission to leave as the ship's whistle sounded, announcing departure. It was funny. It was horrible. It was straight out of Kafka.

Some nine years later, in October 1933, Balanchine arrived in New York from France. I don't remember when Mr. B told us this story about his cultural introduction to the United States in the company of Nicholas Nabokov, or what triggered the memory of his brilliant linguistic one-upmanship. I do remember Balanchine's style of storytelling: You never knew quite where he was headed. It was perfectly clear, though, that he relished the telling and enjoyed poking a little fun at himself along with his compatriot.

It seems that Nabokov (the composer cousin of the *Lolita* novelist), himself fairly new to these shores, had been detailed to take the greenhorn under his wing, show him around, and maybe teach him a little English. According to Balanchine, Nabokov comes to get him, says they are going to eat at "wonderful cheap restaurant, American-style," and leads him to a cafeteria. They pick up trays and get on line. A variety of strange food is on display—not the French cuisine Balanchine has left behind. "What should I order?" he asks his friend in Russian. "Just listen," replies Nabokov, "I know how to speak American." When his turn comes, he orders "eggsky-baksky" from the attendant and the same for Balanchine: "eggsky-baksky." They are given plates of bacon and eggs.

The next day, Mr. B goes on, he tells Nabokov that he would like to go back to the wonderful establishment, but this time he will order "eggsky-baksky" for himself, which he does. By the third day—Mr. B's dark eyes are shining as he winds up the tale—he has become an accomplished student of cafeteria lingo. And already he has learned more "American," much *much* more, than Nicholas Vladimirovich. *"Slushad!"* Just listen to me! he tells his friend as they move along the counter. When he catches the attendant's eye, with Olympian confidence Balanchine orders "eggsky-**mit**-baksky." True-blue American from day three.

Mr. B's attitude toward unions was very different from my parents'. As a young girl, my mother worked twelve hours a day in a sweat shop on 14th Street making flowers for ladies' hats. She told me how she and the other girls had once heard terrible noises outside. They had leaned out the windows to see a mass of union organizers and workers gathered in the square who were being machine-gunned by strike-breaking police. Mr. B equated "union" with "lazy." When, exhausted from a rehearsal at the School that had gone well over two hours without a break we staged a sit-down, Balanchine looked at us uncomprehending. What was this about? He hadn't told us to stop, had he? Nobody answered. Finally, ashamed of our gutless silence, I cited the union regulations: We were supposed to have a five-minute break every hour. Mr. B muttered "union," and then a proverb in Russian: something something *vgrabu*. Queried, he was happy to translate. "In Russia, we say to young dancer 'You will get all the rest you want—in your *grave.*'" We got the idea that the students at the Imperial Ballet School in St. Petersburg had heard this more than once.

Balanchine could be elitist and egalitarian at once. He prized quirky independent thinking and aesthetic freedom. His unwavering focus on his work was the only predictable thing about him. The man was an amalgam of attributes and attitudes, unreadable at times even to those closest to him. He could be intense, enthusiastic, even passionate, yet he maintained control of his feelings. He had a weird sense of humor and a polyglot imagination. You have to marvel at the catholicity of his undertakings: Hollywood "spectaculars" and Broadway shows spilled out along with avant-garde experiments and classical divertissements. Nothing fazed him and nothing was "beneath" him, as the circus elephants discovered when he calmly choreographed a Stravinsky polka for them. He could pour his energy into a sizzling "Slaughter on Tenth

Avenue" or a full-length *Nutcracker*, a crackling insouciant *Western Symphony* or a miraculously chiseled *Agon*. The very first ballet he made in America for American dancers was the dramatic, deeply romantic *Serenade* to the music of Tchaikovsky. If Balanchine remained a staunch political Conservative, he was just as certainly a theatrical Revolutionary.

At the time of the 1948 election, Balanchine and Maria Tallchief had been married well over two years. Maria was not only American, with a Scotch-Irish lineage inherited, so I heard, from her mother. She was part Indian princess. Aside from her bravura dancing and genuine musicianship, Tallchief's Native American background must have enhanced Maria's attractiveness for Mr. B. At the Osage ceremony that followed their marriage, Balanchine was given a silver and turquoise tribal bracelet that never left his wrist, even after their divorce. It signaled his identity as an adopted son, a Native American, and you can't get more American than that. In his informing, beautifully balanced biography of the choreographer, Bernard Taper tells us that Maria's Indian heritage "charmed" Balanchine. In 1947, the year following their marriage, Taper recounts, "he crossed the country by train to join her in Los Angeles . . . and to work with Stravinsky on *Orpheus*," and became excited "when the train, passing through Oklahoma, went by an Indian reservation. 'Look, those are my new relatives!' he proudly told Nicolas Nabokov, with whom he was making the trip, and then for hours regaled Nabokov with Indian lore—all this in Russian, of course."[2]

Henry Wallace didn't win in 1948, Truman did. Of course, Mr. B could not know that his "pinko" little radical was perched on the horns of a dilemma. Split two ways. *My* parents looked askance at my flirtation with "reactionary" culture, the imperialist regime that had nurtured Russian ballet. Almost all our teachers had been trained at the Imperial Ballet Academy. One of our secretaries at the School of American Ballet was the daughter of a general who had been commended by the Tsar; the other was a princess. Madame Davidova, she of the dark eyes and dark suntan who came to watch rehearsals in her pearls and furs, was a countess. I gobbled up the Russian novels and short stories in my father's collection. Pushkin, Dostoevsky, Chekhov, Tolstoy. I was enchanted by the objects displayed in the Fifth Avenue windows of *A la Vieille Russie*: the tortoise-shell and silver cosmetic boxes, the Tsarina's Fabergé Easter egg, the miniature icons, triptychs framing holy figures with arched Byzantine eyebrows, golden skin, and almond eyes. These exotic things belonged to a lost world. They were seductively beautiful, drenched in romance, perhaps especially so to a teenager who was one of the "red-diaper" babies born in the Depression.

It would be many years before I came to read Thoreau's great essay which begins "That government is best that governs least," and recognized Mr. Balanchine's political philosophy in a nutshell. I had of course practiced my own Flatbush form of civil disobedience when my boss asked me to remove my Wallace button. I'd like to say for the record that, so far as I know, Mr. Balanchine never exposed any colleagues to the House Un-American Activities Committee, or cost theater associates their jobs, as I heard Jerry Robbins and Leonard Bernstein both did after being interrogated. I suppose there wouldn't have been much point in threatening Mr. B. His Russian cronies tended toward nostalgia for the *ancien régime*; they were hardly the sort to harbor Marxist tendencies. And *he* wore a turquoise and silver Native American identity bracelet. His file was squeaky clean.

5

An Unexpected Turn

*I*T'S PITCH DARK on stage and a cold draft is circulating from somewhere beyond the wings. The music has mounted to a furious climax and crashed into silence. I'm on the floor breathing hard, dripping sweat and chilled, sprawled among a mass of bodies. We've done a lot of crouching and jumping, running this way and that before the final dive to the ground. The Prince has hacked his way offstage, pulling the royal maiden after him. The evil wizard is slain, his creatures felled. Vanquished demons are piled in heaps, limbs overlapping, monstrous shapes ranged in a rough semi-circle. We are positioned as close as possible to the backdrop and side-drops, as rehearsed, so as to leave downstage and center stage clear. The Firebird remains, poised, motionless, her plumes quivering in a cone of golden light. And, just as in rehearsal, our eyes are riveted on Tallchief, watching for the moment she begins her difficult final variation.

We premiered Stravinsky's *Firebird* in November 1949, just thirteen months after the New York City Ballet crystallized out

43

of Ballet Society. Balanchine had completely re-choreographed it. The musical score had been commissioned by Serge Diaghilev, who originally asked Anatole Liadov to undertake the work. When he learned that the older composer would require a year to complete it, Diaghilev gave the commission to the young Stravinsky. *L'Oiseau de Feu* opened at the Paris Opera on June 25, 1910, with scenery and costumes by Alexander Golovin (except for the Firebird and the Princess, whose costumes were designed by painter Leon Bakst) and the whole lavish spectacle was staged by Michel Fokine. In 1926, a new production was mounted by Diaghilev; retaining the Fokine choreography but completely redesigned by Nathalie Gontcharova.

In the original production, the role of the Firebird was created by the legendary Tamara Karsavina. I'd seen pictures of her as the maiden who dances with Nijinsky in *Le Spectre de la Rose*, as the stunningly beautiful court lady in *Pavillon d'Armide*, as the barefoot seductress in *Salome*.[1] On our first trip to London, just a few months away, the company would be invited to attend a "lesson" on pantomime exquisitely performed by that same Karsavina, who was then in her eighties. Balanchine had made it clear that this was a special treat, and no pilgrim approached the rocky niche at Lourdes with deeper humility than we young Americans approached the platform on which we would behold the living Karsavina.

The great ballerina arrived precisely on time. She was tiny, dressed in gray with a longish skirt and she looked very very old. After a few words of welcome in English, she launched straightaway into her demonstration. Turning into a girl of seventeen, she showed the formal movements that denote Shyness, Love, an Engagement. Before each segment, she briefly explained what she was about to do. *This* was the movement—arms raised above the head, hands circling one another—that meant "Dance" itself. *This* was "Refusal," wrists crossed in front of the body, fists clenched, chin up, eyes adamant. *This* was "Baby," tender cradling of invisible child at bosom. Now, one after the other, she would perform the seven degrees of "Fright"—from the shudder of a mild startle

Maria Tallchief and Francisco Moncion in *Firebird* (1949). Photo: George Platt Lynes, © Estate of George Platt Lynes. Jerome Robbins Dance Division, The New York Public Library for the Performing Arts, Astor, Lenox and Tilden Foundations.

to outright flight, running across the platform, shaking arms extended in front, head turned back, eyes blind with fear. You could not take your eyes from her. This beautiful, wizened old woman was whatever she wanted you to think she was. And she had something else as rare: the exceptional modesty of those souls who know that they can charm and delight whenever they so choose.

At the time of our *Firebird* premiere, we were tickled to learn that in the 1926 production of that ballet, the role of the evil wizard Kostchei, the Firebird's antagonist, was played by a twenty-one-year-old Georgi Balanchivadze—that is, by none other than Mr. B himself. In our production, Maria Tallchief danced the part of the exotic bird and handsome, intense Francisco Moncion was the Russian Prince who, with the help of the Firebird, frees an enchanted Princess and her attendant maidens from Kostchei's powerful spells. Arlene Croce, meditating on the series of productions that followed the original L'Oiseau de Feu danced by Karsavina, questioned the very idea of such a role: "Yet could anyone then—can anyone now—dance a bird made of fire?" she asked, and pointed to the role's essential challenge: "Unlike the Swan Queen, the Firebird is never at any time human."[2] Looking back, it seems to me that this observation precisely describes Balanchine's purpose: to choreograph a bird of fire, never at any time human. And it was precisely Maria's project to become that flaming inhuman power. Clearly, in the style and complexity of its movement, our Firebird was utterly different from the earlier versions. What remained unchanged was the folktale itself, and Stravinsky's music. Not so the sets.

Marc Chagall had designed the sets and costumes that we were going to use. The front curtain, backdrops, and side panels were marvelously colorful and imaginative. With their childlike upside-down figures, they looked like fantastic illustrations out of a book of Russian fairytales. These hand-painted drops and costumes had lain in storage since 1945 when the American Ballet Theatre had undertaken a revival of the work with choreography by Adolph Bolm. ABT had faithfully reproduced the original pre-Raphaelite atmosphere, complete with captured maidens daintily tossing a golden ball among themselves. But the ballet itself was only minimally successful—it seemed dated—and after a couple of seasons the production was laid to rest. Our fledgling company had acquired the Chagall sets and costumes.

Maybe six or seven weeks before the scheduled opening, a number of outsize theater trunks were hauled over to the City Center and unloaded backstage. I can still see Mr. Balanchine gingerly lifting costumes out of a trunk, shaking them a bit, and selecting a few for dancers to try on. I can almost smell the musty, fungus-like odor they exuded. You could make out dried sweat stains. Had they been cleaned? Word went round that the designs on some of the costumes were painted by Chagall himself—which lent them a certain cachet—but nobody was eager to try on the smelly things. The exhumed "princess" dresses meant for the attendant maidens were handed to the taller girls. The fraying, ripped, beat-up monster outfits were slated for the shorter members of the corps, boys and girls who would represent the slaves of Kostchei. Luckily, as it turned out, the mouldy old things were unusable. Balanchine may have consulted Madame Karinska about the condition of the costumes, because it was decided to use only the sets. We were vastly relieved to hear that new costumes had been ordered; fittings were speedily scheduled at Karinska's, not only for the principal dancers but for all of us. On opening night, my cohorts and I were clad in spiffy new monster outfits.

Now we're strewn about the stage waiting for Maria's final solo to begin. The premiere is almost over. I've danced my heart out. During these long drawn-out moments of reverberating silence, a question gathers in my mind. What am I *doing* here curled up in the dark, shivering? A faceless monster whirled to the outskirts of the stage? Then a sensation replaces the thought: *This is familiar. I know this floor like the back of my hand.*

Ballet Society had periodically performed at the City Center, and each of us in that original company knew the exact location of the holes and grooves in the linoleum where City Opera sets were anchored. Balanchine had mounted *Orpheus* on this very same stage the year before. And the year before that, resplendent in white *tutus*, we had danced Bizet's *Symphony in C* on it, and the Mozart *Symphonie Concertante* in E-Flat: our two classical "white ballets." At no time during these performances had I questioned why I was there. It was an adventure.

As a young member I'd seen the Company take root and grow. I had watched marvelous new ballets come into being, associated with extraordinary dancers. In 1946, Mr. B had staged Paul Hindemith's *Four Temperaments for Piano and Orchestra* using a palette of movement recalling Mary Wigman (the modern-dance exponent

Todd Bolender executing movements from the "Phlegmatic" variation in *The Four Temperaments* (period of its Ballet Society production, probably late 1940s). Collage from contact photos by George Platt Lynes, © Estate of George Platt Lynes.

of German Expressionism), along with pointe work and classical technique—a startling combination. *Four Ts*, with its flamboyant costumes and backdrop by Kurt Seligmann (a painter known also for his comprehensive study on the history of magic), came across as a seriously modernist work, yet Balanchine must have challenged, or maybe amused himself by inventing a quasi-humorous treatment of the medieval "humours" or "temperaments."

Each of the four principal dancers had been selected to represent one of these personality types. This season it was Herbert Bliss (Melancholic), Todd Bolender (Phlegmatic), Maria Tallchief (Sanguinic), and Tanaquil Le Clercq (Choleric). While each of them mirrored the modality they'd been chosen to represent, Todd, in particular, elegantly conveyed the satire built into his "Phlegmatic" variation. Todd had studied with Hanya Holm, a follower of Mary Wigman, and Balanchine, with his genius for drawing upon a given dancer's idiosyncratic way of moving, had capitalized on Bolender's natural liquidity. Todd's every movement in "Phlegmatic" suggested a cross between the boneless straw-man in *The Wizard of Oz* and some dismal character plucked out of Gogol.

Most significant, from my own point of view, Mr. B had staged *Concerto Barocco* for us. It was Balanchine's sublime visualization of the Bach double violin concerto that made me vow to study ballet seriously. I wanted to dance those steps to that music, perhaps more than I'd wanted anything in my life. We danced *Barocco* in plain black tunics against a bare cyclorama—just as it was danced in the Ballet Russe—stripped of the elaborate Eugene Berman backdrop and costumes designed for its earlier incarnation. In this period of aesthetic rigor and forced economies, both the Bach and the Hindemith had sacrificed exterior color and ornament so that movement could be seen in its purest state.

I'd seen Marie-Jeanne and Patricia Wilde as the perfectly matched soloists in the Ballet Russe production of *Barocco*. Marie-Jeanne, with her straight-arrow legs and a torso that yielded like a steel beam in a strong wind, had been able to convey both the purity of line and the sensuality that coursed through the slow second movement, the *pas de deux*. That season I saved up my allowance money and all my spare nickels and dimes to buy the RCA Victor recording—Yehudi Menuhin and Georges Enesco on 78 rpm—and listened to it non-stop until my good Jewish-atheist mother despaired of my obsession with this "church music."

I wasn't the only one who wondered how Balanchine could conceive such utterly different works in so short a period. The mathematical and poignant *Barocco*, the ultra-modernist *Four Ts*, the ritual drama of *Orpheus*, the abstract "white" ballets. Now he'd completely reshaped Stravinsky's *Firebird*, a traditional "story ballet," a Russian fairytale with its good and evil forces clearly marked, its adventurous hero and captive princess, its monsters and maidens, its mercurial magical bird. Between the darkness on stage and the vast blackness of the house, I can make out the orchestra pit and the dimly lit podium where the conductor's staccato gestures have been replaced by a hovering baton. In the hush, it sweeps down to cue in the harp and the first plaintive notes of the *Berceuse*. Now the cone of light flickers; Maria has begun to move.

Only it is not Maria, until very recently a principal dancer with the Ballet Russe de Monte Carlo. Neither is it Mr. Balanchine's wife, the proud Osage princess with the flashing smile. Nor is it the studious Maria, serious in practice clothes, absorbing Mr. B's directions with a kind of earnest determination. And it is not our tireless *prima ballerina*, Tallchief the perfectionist, who during rehearsal has found it problematic, at times impossible, to execute a perfect double turn *à la seconde*—that is, pivoting twice around on one leg with the other extended at right angles to the body—at the climax of this extremely demanding variation. This is no ballerina but an enchanted bird, glowing and sparkling and fluttering in a blinding rose-amber spotlight. A magical being exposed in a private moment, casting its spell in a precisely calculated series of steps, and in some way forcing you to feel the depth of its solitude, the piercing singularity of its existence.

This dazzling creature now arrives downstage center and we watch, almost as blinded as she is by the spotlight, her preparation for the problematic double turn, the nerve-wracking turn she has practiced and practiced and sometimes missed in rehearsal.

Tallchief as the Firebird. Photo: George Platt Lynes, © Estate of George Platt Lynes. Jerome Robbins Dance Division, The New York Public Library of Performing Arts, the Astor, Lenox and Tilden Foundations.

The suspense is almost palpable. You can sense the tension, not only on the darkened stage and in the frozen stance of the figures crowding the wings during this first performance, but issuing from the black hole of the audience as well.

Then a kind of miracle takes place. We see not two, not a double, but *three* slow floating turns suspended in amber light. A *triple!* A perfectly balanced triple turn *à la seconde*: one leg spinning slowly on pointe, the other raised high at the side, straight as a sword, arms like wing-tips raised in an oval above the head. During these moments time has stopped; the flamboyant figure revolving in the dark seems to have transcended the realm of stagecraft and become a principle made visible. In its easy equilibrium, the luminous turning body has become an emblem of the motion-driven universe, is itself the central, timeless, continuously creating "point of the turning world." The house, having held its collective breath, now explodes into ecstatic "Bravos!!" as the bird dissolves into the downstage wing, back deeply bent, arms fluttering behind, fingertips sparkling, flickering spasmodically in the golden sphere of light.

In that November of 1949, it took Mr. B a bare three weeks to choreograph the entire ballet anew and rehearse all the parts. He had re-conceived the role of the Firebird to fit Maria's particular movement, musicality, technique—and speed. Fokine's sinuous voluptuary was now transposed to a brilliant whirling creature moving virtually everywhere at once. A bird of fire, an inhuman power. It didn't occur to me at the time that the magical Firebird of Russian folklore, the unique and solitary and splendid bird who could cast enchantments and undo spells, that the flaming, phoenix-like creature so vibrantly rendered by Tallchief in that first matchless performance was, in effect, a paradigm of Balanchine's own creative genius.

6

A Prodigal Fall

$\mathcal{M}$R. B RECAST *Prodigal Son* for our 1950/1951 season, and spent some time rehearsing Frank Moncion and Yvonne Mounsey in the principal roles. *Prodigal* was another "story ballet," set to music by Prokofieff and based on the well-known parable in the Bible. Like *Firebird*, it was an oldie from the Diaghilev days, with a black-outlined backdrop and richly colored costumes designed by Georges Rouault. In this case however, Balanchine himself had done the original choreography. And he had contributed a spectacular new dimension to the tale.

The story in the Gospel of Saint Luke tells about a father who divides his inheritance between two sons. The older son stays home, husbands the land and thrives; the younger takes his portion and heads for the fleshpots. Far from home he falls into bad company, wastes his substance in "riotous living," and is reduced to feeding swine in a land devastated by famine. Starving, the boy decides to return home, confess that he has sinned against heaven and his father, and ask if he may be allowed to work for him as a hired servant.

Seeing his younger son approaching from afar, the father runs to meet him, falls on his neck rejoicing and orders a great celebration. As might be expected, the older brother who has been laboring in the fields is angry when he finds the household feasting and making merry at the prodigal's return. Why kill the fatted calf to welcome a wastrel, he asks, when his own hard work has not been acknowledged? The parable concludes with the father assuring the older son that he treasures his fidelity: "Son, thou art ever with me," he says, "and all that I have is thine." But, he counters, "thy brother was dead and is alive; and was lost, and is found."

It was not that Balanchine departed completely from the story as told in the gospel. He'd replaced the figure of the older brother with two loving sisters. In a more radical departure, he had reimagined the father's response when the Prodigal returns. Actually reversed it. Where the parable in Luke has the father falling on the repentant son's neck, kissing him, clothing him, calling for music, dancing, a feast, Balanchine substituted a motionless Patriarch, a grave holy icon. As for the rest of the ballet, he followed the narrative as given—but in his own way, with the prodigal's self-destruction occurring as present action. He rendered visible what was only suggested in the original, colored in the empty spaces, so to speak. What Balanchine revealed in astonishing depth by this maneuver was the extent of the son's degradation. It showed his descent into swinish behaviors and the company of thieves. It fleshed out the way he had "spent his substance in riotous living," devoured his portion "with harlots."

Mr. B revived the ballet for us toward the end of February 1950. Jerome Robbins had recently joined the Company as both dancer and choreographer and Balanchine immediately cast Jerry as the young Prodigal and Maria Tallchief as the Siren who seduces, corrupts, and fleeces him after a series of orgiastic revels suggesting the heyday of Sodom and Gomorrah. The boy ends up in rags, half naked. In the closing scene, he drags his chastened body across the stage and crawls to the feet of his father who stands motionless before his tent. During the final stirring measures of music, the Patriarch, dressed in a golden robe, does not bend to help his son but remains majestically upright, arms outstretched, as the boy climbs up his body to be enfolded at last.

In the season following the premiere, Frank, who was larger and more muscular than Jerry, replaced him in the title role. Yvonne, who had trained as a dancer in South Africa and was larger and more muscular than Tallchief, took over the part of the sultry vamp. This was a role made famous by one of the most cherished teachers at the School of American Ballet, Madame Felia Doubrovska. Like Doubrovska, Yvonne was tall and commanding. She was taller than Maria to begin with and her height was exaggerated by a headpiece almost a foot high in length. Also like Doubrovska, Yvonne had long shapely legs, a high bosom, and a strong willowy back. She may not have been quite as lithe and slithery as her Russian forerunner, but Yvonne was a natural for the part and you could tell she enjoyed dancing it.

I wasn't in this ballet but had taken advantage of a long break between my own rehearsals to relax for awhile and see what was going on in the other studio. It's always a pleasure to observe other people hard at work, and a number of us settled on the bench in front of the mirror with knee-warmers over our tights and towels around our necks to watch Mr. B rehearse Frank and the guys in the Banquet Scene. This episode contained the dramatic climax of the action. It required stamina, strong muscles, and precision timing on the part of every dancer. The Prodigal has to scramble to the top of a long black table (strongly recalling the Passover table of the Last Supper) that the guys are tilting higher and higher until it's at a precarious 45-degree angle from the floor. At the apex the boy, seen in profile, throws his head back, his left hand at the side of a wide-open mouth, the right arm thrust straight ahead, palm flexed upward—the "trumpet call" for help. After a moment's freeze, he's thrown violently off balance and tumbles to the floor where he is attacked and the clothes ripped from his body.

The guys now turn into spiders, paired off back-to-back, spines pressed hard against each other, elbows linked. They skitter around in circles, two-headed and four-legged, knees bent in a wide *plié*, scuttle from one end of the room to the other and finally make off to the sides. It's brilliant! A *tour de force*. A deliciously loathsome sight. The Siren snatches a last ornament from the boy's neck and disappears. The despoiled Prodigal lies where he has fallen, curled up like a foetus.

At this point we see Balanchine walk over to Moncion and say something to him. Frank uncurls and gets to his feet. Balanchine says something else, seems to be coaching him. Frank does the last fall a couple of times, then gets up and waits. The "spiders" are unhitched now, leaning back against the barre, blotting the sweat from arms, face, and neck. Mr. B just stands there in the middle of the floor with his back to the mirror and a kind of vacant look on his face. Nothing is happening. After quite a long pause he snaps back, as it were. And then—most unusual—he begins to tell a story right in the middle of rehearsal. He is addressing Frank but everyone in the room can hear him:

"You know," he recalls in a voice that is low-key but very clear, "When I do *Prodigal Son* for Diaghilev, Lifar is favorite. He is golden boy. Can do nothing wrong. Everybody say he is *wonderful!* all the time *wonderful!* Sometimes he is dancing very bad," Mr. B goes on in a reasonable tone, "but for Diaghilev, Lifar was star. He is god. We make *Prodigal Son* just for Lifar" (here Balanchine sniffs, pauses) "and I make step he will not do." The room goes deadly quiet. "'Here you stand straight, Lifar, very straight,' I tell him, 'and fall on your back.' He will not do this. He is afraid. He tells me, he tells Diaghilev, 'No, this will hurt my back.' So now Diaghilev wants me to change, make new step. Make something else."

There cannot have been a soul in that rehearsal room who didn't know that Diaghilev had been Lifar's lover. Now Mr. B peers around and sees us all paying rapt attention. What happened? Frank wants to know. "Wa-a-a-l," drawls our choreographer, "I *explain*. I tell Lifar it will *not* hurt, not at all. I will show you how to do, I say to Lifar, because this is what I want. So I show him. I show him how to do." Balanchine makes a gesture, his arm moving from vertical to horizontal. "I fall flat on my back!" We all stare.

Somebody blurts out, "Didn't it hurt?"

"Oh yes," says Mr. Balanchine, "hurt like hell! But I had to do only once and Lifar, he must do *every night!*"

I got up the nerve once, to ask Mr. B why the father in *Prodigal* doesn't help the boy at the end. Why does he just stand there while the boy crawls painfully up the path to the tent? In the Bible story, I reminded him, the father runs to embrace the son. Why didn't Mr. B at least have the father go to meet him and help him, instead of letting him drag himself along with his cane? The boy was sorry, I pointed out; he was crippled and starving. Didn't the father feel compassion? Why was he so stern and unbending? Balanchine heard me out and when I finally sputtered to a stop, he told me in firm tones: "No. Father does not move. He is like God. Boy must come to *him.*"

Dr. Mel Kiddon administering required shots to me before European tour.
Photographer unknown, from author's collection.

7

On Tour, 1952

CATALONIAN EXTREMES

THE NEW YORK CITY BALLET departed for Barcelona on April 7, 1952, for its first European "grand tour," and flew home exactly five months later on the seventh of September after a week of performances at the Berlin Städtische Oper. This trip was longer and more varied than our first venture over the Atlantic, a summer engagement at Covent Garden two years earlier. In 1950, we'd spent almost two months in a postwar London that had suffered constant heavy bombardment and was still suffering severe shortages. I tasted horse meat and ate rabbit stew for the first time. Some of us roomed together in the attic of a gloomy town house in South Kensington run by a Russian émigré couple, and rode the Underground in to work. The floors below us were crammed with dark mahogany furniture and bookcases, not too thoroughly dusted. Descending from the top floor of 23 Weatherby Gardens, you could see moth-eaten animal skins on the floors; a bell jar full of stuffed birds stared down from the top of a closet. It was a spooky "digs," especially after I borrowed a copy of Bram Stoker's *Dracula* from one of the bookcases and fell unresisting into a realm of Transylvanian castles, howling werewolves, the undead cloistered in ruined chapels, and vampires gorged with blood in the London of an earlier century.

All of us experienced the aftermath of war in ways we had not, back in the States: destroyed buildings left half-standing, acres of rubble, the continued food rationing, a kind of brittle cheerfulness in the demeanor of people we met. But we were also invited to tea at Windsor Castle, to a champagne party at Lady Astor's town house, and we attended that magical performance of pantomime by Tamara Karsavina. Even more heartening, we found a ballet audience at Covent Garden Opera House that not only knew and loved the classical repertoire, but one that greeted our unfamiliar new works with an enthusiasm verging at times on delirium. British balletomanes crowded the stage door after matinee and evening performances and seemed to know every one of us by name. It was heady stuff. We sobered up, however, before heading home. After Covent Garden, we briefly played Manchester and Croydon, grim manufacturing towns, and Liverpool, a working seaport. Outside London we found welcoming audiences, but no delirium.

The 1952 tour was more than a "feeler." We were booked at major opera houses in Spain, France, Italy, Switzerland, the Netherlands, and Germany. We were returning with brand new ballets to a friendly, familiar London and we'd been asked to perform in Scotland at the Edinburgh Festival. During that engagement, as I recall, the entire company was invited on its "dark night" to view the ceremonial "Tattoo" at Edinburgh Castle. I remember us standing three-deep at the edge of the parade ground where we saw the marshaling of the clans with bagpipes and drums, marveled at the stature and "swank" of the nearly seven-foot Major Domo and heard the solitary Piper, perched high on a spotlighted battlement, send his eerie music skirling into the dark. A stirring, unforgettable experience—and germinal it would seem, to two Balanchine ballets.

For a good many of us though, our first stop on that 1952 tour was unsettling, even shocking. It could be argued that discipline is the first fact of existence for professional dancers. We've undergone years of rigorous training and we recognize discipline when we see it. During our weeks in Barcelona, we discerned its presence in modes that were peculiarly Spanish, some uniquely regional. Extreme discipline was fundamental to the blood ceremonies of the *corrida*, the life and death rigor of the bull-ring; it was present in the mathematical, asymmetrical heel-tapping and hand-clapping of tubercular flamenco gypsies; it was appallingly evident in the public self-flagellation of hooded monks during the Good Friday Procession.

Beyond these aesthetic and ascetic disciplines, there was a visible military presence in the city. Barcelona was a seaport known for constant uprisings; a political prison stood atop nearby Monthuïc. I discovered this the hard way. One cool Monday morning I set off on a solitary hike, using my BOAC bag for a backpack. It held a bottle of water, some lunch, my wallet, my passport, a camera, my lipstick, and an orange. A few Kleenex, just in case. Although a performance was scheduled for that evening, we had the whole day to ourselves; no class and no rehearsal. Someone had said there was a breathtaking view from the cliffs halfway up the mountain, and I was planning to have my lunch overlooking the harbor far below. I'd passed the outskirts of the city, and begun to climb a steep winding road when I saw a wooden sign that said *"No pasa"* in large black letters, and something *"muerte"* underneath. Almost simultaneously, two shots rang out overhead. I got off that road real fast, scrambled into the hillside trees and brush, and ended up scratched and breathless on a rock overlooking the ocean. When two soldiers appeared, armed with enormous rifles, I knew they were going to shoot me and throw me over the cliff. Sudden death. Panic. And guilt: *Who'll take my place in "Swan Lake" tonight?* In desperation I plunged into the BOAC bag, found the orange, and held it out to them as an offering.

Pedro and José turned out to be pussycats. Both were swarthy, dark-eyed, thin and small, which is why their guns looked so large.

Barcelona (1952). Pedro and José on Monthuïc. Snapshot from author's collection.

They knew maybe ten words of English between them and I had no Spanish, but somehow they made me understand that the road was forbidden, that they were guards at the prison—*politico*—up there on the mountain, and that they were far from their homes in the North. They wanted to know what I was doing in Barcelona and, after seeing my little photo of Central Park with surrounding buildings, shyly assured me that they would love to visit New York, pointing with smiles to the picture and themselves. After we socialized for awhile and shared the orange, they escorted me back to the road. I still have a snapshot of those two sweet guys who didn't throw me over the cliff.

In general, the people we encountered outside the theater seemed extremely poor to young American dancers. The workmen quietly went about their business, could be surprisingly sweet-tempered and helpful, but broadcast an air of resignation, at least to this onlooker. Once or twice we saw men enjoying a drinking game: how high can you squirt the liquid from the wineskin and still catch the stream in your mouth? Without losing a drop. During Holy Week we didn't see such games; they were crowding with their families into the Cathedral and the churches. Whole families observed Holy Thursday by making a silent pilgrimage to seven churches, one after the other. For many of us, Catalonian Barcelona presented a culture of contradictions, a study in social, economic, and political extremes.

Mr. Balanchine was well aware of serious objections to performing in Generalissimo Franco's Spain. Nora Kaye, who had left the American Ballet Theatre to join us, refused outright at first to dance in this infamously repressive dictatorship, but Mr. B had his own priorities. He knew that his dancers were unaccustomed to a steeply raked stage. It takes practice to run lightly uphill, to put on the brakes when you're executing a series of fast turns downhill, as in *Serenade*. It takes time to adjust to a whole new set of balances during partnered lifts and pirouettes. You must learn to "lean back" on thin air when you're on pointe facing the audience, so you don't fall on your face. Your whole body begins to appreciate the physics of "upstage" and "downstage" as never before.

Balanchine needed Barcelona because he cared about Paris. He wanted his dancers to shine in Paris. More than anywhere else, he was hoping his new company would create the strongest possible impression, perhaps become a *succès fou*, a smash hit, when we opened at the Opéra. Cosmopolitan Paris knew George Balanchine. In the twenties, Parisians had applauded his first stunning modernist works for Diaghilev's Russian Ballet. More recently they had seen the premiere of *Palais de Cristal*, the Bizet symphony Balanchine choreographed for the Paris Opera Ballet before it became our own *Symphony in C*. I think Mr. B was hoping to take the city by storm, deliver a sensational *coup de théâtre*. On the other hand, we were not yet the polished Company we would become. It's just possible that he didn't want us to embarrass him. In either case, there was one overriding reason to open in Barcelona. It so happened that the stage of the Gran Teatro del Liceo had precisely the same rake, the same angle of slant, as the stage of the Paris Opera, the Palais Garnier. So we spent five grueling weeks of rehearsals and performances learning to dance on a stage built for opera, for pantomimes, for pageants and parades—for everything but strenuous Balanchine ballets. Like the Paris Opera House, the stage of the Liceo had a tilt of roughly one inch to every three feet.

The steep rake wasn't the only problem. Performances *began* at 11 P.M., just about the time the closing curtain would be coming down in New York. You got to the theater at 9:30 to put on makeup and do warm-ups at the barre, and you waited until after the performance to have dinner. We were pretty hungry, maybe a little lightheaded by 2 A.M., and quickly learned to take advantage of the afternoon *siesta*. The theater accommodated the rich and powerful, the rich and gently bred, and a class of patrons more modestly endowed. The house, like the old Metropolitan Opera House in New York, had the shape of a giant horseshoe. It was baroquely ornate, a gilt and plush affair with richly appointed tiers of boxes and circle upon circle of curving balconies. Each of these began and ended at the proscenium arch that framed the stage. The grandees' private boxes at the Liceo were at stage level and at one tier above. Splendid wrought-iron grilles separated the boxes from the backstage, and allowed the occupants to observe what was going on before the curtain went up. Faces peered through them during warm-up, watching us like animals in a zoo.

The highest circles, of course, were the cheapest and not very plush. Someone, maybe the stage manager, pointed out a daredevil who occupied the very last seat in the very first row of the topmost circle—the balcony squashed against the roof that the Brits call "the gods." Well, he didn't actually "occupy" the seat. Whoever had that place could see the show only when he planted one foot on the proscenium arch and held tight to the balcony railing so that he could look down at the stage. We were scared to death that during the performance one night a body would plummet into the abyss below.

Backstage was not so grand. We changed into practice clothes and costumes in stone-cold subterranean dressing rooms that you reached by climbing down narrow stone stairways to one of three basement levels under the stage. These gave access to a labyrinth of cells, mostly without running water, each lit by a single hanging bulb that cast 25 to 40 watts of dismal light. At the City Center we applied our greasepaint and eyeshadow in front of mirrors ringed with bright lights. Radiators sent out heat on cold days. There were sinks in the dressing rooms and a bathroom on each floor. Backstage at the Liceo, the men who hauled the trunks and handled the sets were very like the military guards on Montheuil: swarthy, small, undernourished, and eager to please. Ruth Sobotka, the Austrian dancer and artist who would design the costumes for Jerry Robbins's shocker, *The Cage*, could speak a little Spanish. Through her we learned that the stagehands all worked three jobs, starting at 4 A.M. when they hauled crates in the market. They lived outside the city, rode the tram in and back home every day, and brought their lunches with them: bread, a bit of chocolate, sometimes a wedge of cheese. I have no idea when they slept, other than during *siesta* when the entire city shut down for hours.

The dapper, handsome man with black eyes, wearing black tie and a formal dinner jacket stood backstage every single night. He told us his name was Antonio.

"What do you do, Antonio?"
"What I do?"
"Yes. Why do you stand backstage through all the ballets? Why don't you sit out front?"
The good-looking man smiles. His eyes light with understanding. He brings his hands together, palms turned upward.
"Oh! Why I stand here while you dance? Ha! I am here to catch BOMB!" He pronounces both "b's" in "bomb."

Antonio pantomimes catching sight of a large, about-to-explode grenade, fielding it in cupped hands like a football, and zigzagging toward the nearest wing with it hugged close to his chest. He's joking. He's joking?

Barcelona was a hotbed of rebellion but it was also a bastion of faith, especially evident during the week preceding Easter. The great Gothic Cathedral rises above the hovels of the poor, its cavernous interior twinkling with candles. On Holy Thursday, families

made their rounds together while we rehearsed. On Good Friday a
seemingly endless procession began at the doors of the Cathedral,
led by riders in colorful costumes trying to calm white horses jerk-
ing at the bit. It looked like they'd pranced out of a medieval tap-
estry. The procession wound along the *Ramblas de las Flores* where
the women who keep the flower stalls nurse infants hidden behind
thick shawls. This day, the grand boulevard was hemmed in by a
mass of somber onlookers. Making my way from the Pensión Cat-
alonia to the theater that Friday afternoon, I heard flutes, and then
drums beating in slow funeral rhythm, a dirge. I wriggled to the
front of the crowd, holding tightly to my practice-clothes bag, and
saw a waxen bewreathed Christ-figure floating slowly down the
Ramblas. The life-size figure lay prone in a glass coffin, lifted high
over their heads by pall-bearers. Cohorts of monks in slit-eyed Ku
Klux Klan hoods followed, some in black, some in purple, some in
white, all marching barefoot. There were penitents, wrists mana-
cled and ankles dragging chains, and a group of flagellants, with
whips. Silent and intense, the onlookers pressed forward to see the
parade of the religious. The collective mood recalled the intensity
and passion of the gypsies at the *Macareña*. The silences.

The *Macareña* was a little hot-box of gaiety. When our performance was over and makeup off, a bunch of us would head over to
the seedy old café to eat, drink, unwind, and take in some honest-
to-god Flamenco dancing and music. There were no tablecloths at
the *Macareña* but there was lots of talent. All the waiters sang and
danced or coaxed staccato rhythms from the guitar. For a shot glass
of brandy they would dance into a frenzy. Whirling, stamping,
clapping, with proud spines and dervish eyes, they'd toss off the
firewater and retreat coughing—uncontrollable tubercular hack-
ing—only to reappear and ask us to dance with them. And oh! how
we danced! Wild, released from discipline, streaming sweat and delight as if we hadn't spent the entire day and night on our feet.

The women came out to dance solo in long skirts and black
mantillas. There was one plump gypsy who was the empress of
the *Macareña*. She wore an ivory-colored mantilla, a low-cut dress,
and looked to be in her fifties. When she came out, the waiters

cleared extra space for her to dance in. I had never seen such a back! Such an arrogant carriage; such exaggerated disdain. Such a swirl of skirt! Never seen a mantilla manipulated as an incredibly sexual come-on. Never heard castanets clicking like a cosmic code, heels tapping out algorithms with mathematical complexity. When the guitarist came a bit later to play at our table, some of the women sat down with us and accompanied his music with clapping. We tried to follow their irregular system of hand-claps and foot-stamps, but though we could pick up the rhythms without too much trouble, we never knew when exactly to stop. It was a game. They always ended the clapping at the same time, all together, and grinned when we realized we'd been outsmarted once again.

It was impossible to be in Barcelona in springtime and not attend a *corrida*, at least once. Of all the contradictions I experienced, it was the bullfight that generated the most excruciating set of extremes. It was a bloody massacre and an arena of grace. I saw Litre, one of the great matadors, kneel on both knees with his back to the gate waiting for his bull to be loosed, the crowd roaring at his nerve. After the *banderillas* pierced the hide and left the creature streaming blood, he swept the enraged animal through a series of perfect *veronicas*, cape swirling between them like a great red poppy, before heading in *over the horns* for the kill. I heard myself chanting *Olé! Olé!!* along with the crowd at each perfect turn: the slender matador, figure arched, motionless but for the arm holding the short red cape; the confused, bleeding, doomed, charging bull.

At the Gran Teatro del Liceo, we were accorded a "gala" on closing night. It was unexpected and it was amazing. As we took our bows after the last ballet, thoughts already turned to packing up, looking ahead to the next stop on the tour, the front curtain continued to remain open. It would not come down. Suddenly, thousands of flowers began to rain down on the house and stage until fragrant piles of blossoms were heaped everywhere. And while they were still floating down, the applause still echoing in the house, a flight of white doves was loosed from that highest balcony, the circle of "the gods," to soar out and across, back and forth, up and down through the falling petals.

8

On Tour, 1952

ON THE TENTH OF MAY the Company opened in Paris for a single gala night at the Opera House. For the remainder of our stay, from the eleventh to the fifteenth of May, we would move into the smaller Champs Élysées theater just off the Rond Point on the Avenue Montaigne. We were scheduled to dance in Florence, Lausanne, and Zurich after this engagement, and then return to Paris for a few weeks in June. Two years earlier, between our closing at Covent Garden and opening in Manchester, we'd been given a week off near the end of August. Dancers, musicians, stage managers, conductors all whirled off, dispersed like chaff in the wind, many of us flying from London to Gay Paree. The city was pretty empty, deserted in favor of the seaside during the hot weeks. I, for one, spent the first days in Paris sight-seeing and eating rich food—and sincerely regretting it when the sudden change of cuisine turned my stomach to water. Sight-seeing was over but I did manage to drag myself to a summer performance of Mozart's *Magic Flute*, and while the production itself was less than inspiring, to put it mildly, I was impressed by the elegance and grandeur of the Opera House.

I don't know when the old Palais Garnier changed its name to Théâtre National de l'Opéra, but in 1952 it was the same spacious structure on the Place de l'Opéra that I remembered, surrounded by shops and second-story "outlets" that sold expensive Swiss watches, Chanel and Balanciaga perfumes, at cut-rate prices. The entrance hall of the Opéra contained the famous grand staircase and upstairs there was a musty little one-room museum where you could find souvenirs of ancient celebrities who had performed there: someone's satin shoe perhaps, or a feather from a costume hat; autographed programs and faded brown photographs from long ago, under glass. All melted out of memory like the snows of yesteryear. We discovered that the stage of the Paris Opera magically opened up at the rear onto the *Foyer de la danse*, a gilded space with columns and mirrors and crystal chandeliers. Originally planned as an elegant chamber where opera dancers could meet gentleman admirers after the performance, it now served as an extension of the stage for elaborate productions. And it was a swell place to have your photograph taken in costume!

Backstage there were evil-smelling latrines from the middle ages; and it was immediately apparent that the stage floor had the same steep rake we had trained for in Barcelona. Just for the record, I want to say that New York City Ballet's opening night in Paris was truly a marvelous occasion: Not one of us, all the way from the stars and soloists down to the lowest, clumsiest, greenest member of the corps, fell down. The weeks at the Gran Liceo had paid off. Not only were we able to negotiate the rake; every one of us danced as if our lives depended on it. And according to the papers we made a strong impression, if not an immediate *succès fou*.

On the following night we opened at the Théâtre des Champs Élysées. Bizet's *Symphony in C* was scheduled as the last ballet on the program. "Bizet," with its four contrasting movements and exuberant full-cast-on-stage finale, was one of our showpieces. It

Milberg, *en pointe*, Foyer de la danse at Palais Garnier, Paris (1952).
Photo: William McCracken, author's collection.

Executing a split jump, Foyer de la danse (1952). Photo: William McCracken, author's collection.

never failed to gain an enthusiastic response. Back in Barcelona, we'd known that Mr. B was edgy about Paris. What most of us didn't know was that the theater on the Avenue Montaigne harbored special memories for him. Many of the ballets that established his reputation had seen their first performance at this very same theater. Ballet historian Anatole Chujoy touches on the arrival in Paris of the little group of dancers who had escaped the Soviets. They'd completed a brief tour of summer resorts along the Rhine in Germany and headed for Paris early in the autumn, where the Diaghilev Ballet "was having its annual season at the Théâtre des Champs-Élysées."[1] Ours was still a fledgling company, and Mr. Balanchine knew we would be compared with the vastly more experienced (if vastly more untidy) Paris Opera dancers. And we were closing the first performance at the Champs Élysées theater with a ballet set to music by a French composer, a ballet created five years earlier for those same French dancers. In effect, Balanchine had thrown down the gauntlet. He was deliberately inviting comparison.

Fast forward to the night in question, the final ballet on the program, and the triad of viewers—a kind of three-headed, six-eyed monster—inhabiting the stage-right wings. This triple entity, the Guardians of Our Repertoire, stood watching as the opening movement of Bizet's C-major Symphony ended, and the slow strains of the second movement heralded the entrance of corps, soloists, and finally the principal dancers. Mr. B, sniffing compulsively, stood as usual in the downstage right wing that commands the fullest view of the stage. Tall, divinely handsome Lew Christensen, our slave-driving Ballet Master, loomed in the second wing, his face like a thundercloud—a Viking god, Wotan about to loose the lightning bolt. The third wing just upstage of Lew was occupied by Vida Brown, another tough cookie, who recently had been appointed Ballet Mistress. Vida, who was still dancing, had hurried into the third wing between the first and third movements of Bizet, both of which she was in. She stood there in her *tutu*, aghast, tears beginning to trickle down her cheeks. Only the rear wing was clear of onlookers, as it had to be.

The second movement of *Symphony in C* opens with six corps de ballet girls issuing one after the other from that furthermost upstage wing, appearing to float on stage with tiny *pas de bourée* steps on pointe. The music is quiet, the melodic theme poignant, haunting, lyrical. The tempo is *adagio*, a measured leisurely development following the brisk *allegro vivo* of the first movement. After the entrance of the corps and two demi-soloists, the ballerina and her partner appear for the long lovely *pas de deux*, all making their entrance from that same upstage wing.

The first movement had gone off beautifully. The sparkling *allegro* was danced with precision, elegance and *élan*, and concluded without a hitch. It was received with unmistakable enthusiasm. After a slight interval, the second movement began its slow unfolding. Intent on the gliding entrance of long-legged young Tanaquil Le Clercq, led on stage by her partner after the opening measures, it's possible that the audience did not realize that things were out of control. The principal dancers also seemed serenely unaware of what was happening behind them. They were in a world of their own, preparing for an extremely delicate and difficult passage, the climax of the *pas de deux*, which required a sustained balance on the part of the ballerina and the split-second timing of her partner. But behind them, the line of girls in the corps were engaged in a chaotic series of "appear onstage/disappear offstage" fluctuations never choreographed by George Balanchine. The three watchers stationed in the wings couldn't know what was causing the fractured formations, the insane shifts in number, the frenzied darting on and darting off at both sides of the stage. Only the denizens backstage had some idea of the harrowing string of mishaps that triggered the Second Movement Disaster.

The whole miserable farce began with our Wardrobe Mistress, Eudokia Miranova, sending one of the corps de ballet *tutus* out for a trial cleaning. She was taking no chances with the soloists' costumes. Dunya was a practical, skeptical, tyrannical dictator of the wardrobe who had been Anna Pavlova's personal dresser. At this point in time she was small and skinny with wispy white hair, very little English, a thick Russian accent, and a voice that could penetrate stone walls. She stood four feet, eleven inches high and her shoes were size nine—and you didn't talk back to Dunya. You *never* sat down in your costume, and when standing you lightly held up the lowest skirts of your *tutu*—or got a scolding. Her charge was every single costume in the repertoire. She was responsible for having the right costumes hanging ready for the dancers before

Eudokia Miranova ("Dunya"), Wardrobe Mistress, hooking me into costume for *Swan Lake* (early 1950s). Photographer unknown, author's collection.

each ballet. She was responsible for repairing damages, mending, altering, and overseeing necessary cleaning. She was the one who engaged an assistant (her niece) and chose the dressers who helped us in and out of our costumes. Dunya would occasionally request "*tootsie-ketz*" from the management and live in a state of anxiety until her request was honored. After months of puzzling over it (were "*tootsie-ketz*" some kind of Russian delicacy? chewy chocolate kittens?) someone explained to me that she had promised a relative or some old crony *two tickets* to the performance. She was deeply religious, and prayed every night that she be allowed to visit the holy city of Jerusalem before she died.

Dunya knew that Parisians were connoisseurs of fashion, experts in the world of clothing design, and she wanted our costumes to look pristine. But she had to be sure that the professional *nettoyage* in this town could handle a sweat-stained *tutu* without damaging it. So our Wardrobe Mistress tested the theatrical cleaners by sending off one, only one, of the *tutus* worn in *Symphony in C*, a "white ballet." She sent it out from the Opera House and told the cleaners to deliver it to the wardrobe room on the fifth floor of the Champs Élysées theater the following day. And be sure to have it back well before the opening curtain! Maybe the French cleaners had trouble understanding Dunya's thick Russian accent. Maybe they resented her imperial manner. Maybe they returned it by mistake to the Opera House. Or maybe the spirit of Serge Lifar was casting a malevolent spell on us, payback for the fall of the Prodigal Son? Whatever the cause, the *tutu* Dunya sent out never came back. Not that night.

The dressing rooms assigned to the corps de ballet are all the way up on the fourth floor at the *Champs Élysées*. There is no backstage elevator. You have to climb to the fifth floor to get hooked into your costume, then race down four flights to stage level. On this night, with the last intermission over and the audience back in its seats, we hear the sharp opening chords of first movement Bizet. The six of us in second movement pause only to dust on a last bit of powder, then run up to the fifth floor, robes clutched over bodies clad only in pink silk tights and pink satin shoes. The crisp white Bizet *tutus* hanging in double rows in the wardrobe room are identical. There are about thirty of them. Each costume has the wearer's name marked on a label stitched into the bodice. One of the girls in second movement can't find the *tutu* with her name in it. She goes ballistic.

It turns out that someone else is wearing it. Dunya, mouth tight, has hooked the dancer whose costume never came back from the cleaners into this girl's *tutu*. She had no choice; the dancer without a costume was in first movement and had to get on stage pronto. The bereft girl in second movement, now in the same straits, snatches one of the *tutus* still left hanging, gets herself hooked into it and speeds stageward. Meanwhile, Barbara Bocher, another of the six in the second movement, has found her own costume, plucked it off the rack and locked herself into the cramped little bathroom down the hall—but then cannot get it unlocked. She calls out, pounds and hammers on the door, but the wardrobe room has grown too full of confusion for anyone to pay attention. Dancers are yelling at dressers. Dressers are calling for Dunya. Some are near-hysterical. Others are grabbing anyone's *tutu* just to get on stage on time. We are not waiting for the dressers but hurriedly hooking each other up.

I'm in second movement. I hear the slow, long-drawn-out opening notes as I miraculously come upon my very own costume and get hooked in. I whiz down two floors by way of the bannisters, Dunya hoarsely shrieking from above—"DO NOT SLIDE IN TU-*TU*!"—foot it down the last two flights, sprint to the upstage wing and *just* make it on stage. I'm the fifth girl to *bourée* on and the sixth, and last, is right behind me. Heads held high, one arm curved above the head, the other gracefully open, traveling on pointe with tiny steps, we float on stage as if nothing had gone haywire. We are professionals. We are troupers. We don't miss entrances.

Now we become aware that Vida Brown in the upstage wing is gesticulating wildly at us and hissing something over and over. Then we hear it: "GET OFF STAGE!" It dawns on me at this moment that there are not six girls traveling on pointe with tiny steps into a perfectly straight diagonal, but nine. Oops.

Our capable new Ballet Mistress, seasoned by years of touring with Serge Denham's Ballet Russe, has seen only two girls *bourée* onto the stage. Then a gap in the line. Then a serious gap. An emergency. Quick as lightning, she has sent in a few extra bodies to fill the supposed vacancy and with whispers and gestures is indicating where they must go and what they must do. Then the missing dancers arrive and innocently join the overstocked line. One of the replacements does a double-take, and intelligently disappears into the nearest wing on the opposite side of the stage. On our side, the Viking thundercloud in the second wing grows darker, more threatening.

Now there are eight corps de ballet dancers forming the diagonal instead of six and the moment has come for Tanaquil, the principal ballerina, to be led onstage by her partner and glide past our lowered heads. Number six and I, the last of the corps members to come on, tacitly agree to *bourée* quietly offstage as soon as the principals have passed, and the two of us do just that. But we reverse direction almost instantly because we see that three other girls in the lineup have arrived at the same solution and melted into the wings on the other side. Vida emits a squawk . . . and one comes back.

Mr. Balanchine is sniffing non-stop like the Easter Bunny. I'm scared of Lew. I'm scared of Vida. But there are now six girls in the line, just as there should be, and the remainder of the movement goes off perfectly. Tanny does her balance; her partner catches her at the peak moment; we conclude with quiet dignity. Perhaps the audience, accustomed to the untidy performances of their own Opera dancers, didn't notice the number chopping at the beginning. The critics (God bless them!) never mentioned it. Vida Brown, as I recall, had a few things to say to us. What has always remained a mystery is how Bocher got out of the bathroom. Did she break out? Climb over the top partition? Did someone break in and release her? She wouldn't say.

9

On Tour, 1952

VESPA RIDERS

*I*N FLORENCE we were booked at the Teatro Comunale for a couple of weeks in May, a featured event in the city's *Maggio Musicale Fiorentino*, the annual spring music festival. We headed into Italy from Paris, not at all sorry to put behind us the embarrassing onstage mishaps at the Théâtre des Champs Élysées. In time, those very same mistakes and accidents would provide material for a tour song. But off-stage, there had been an equally embarrassing episode that the participants were hoping to keep hush-hush. Unfortunately, it is the nature of such things to leak out, and as our train sped toward Florence's Stazione Centrale the juicy bit of gossip swiftly made its rounds.

It seems that one free afternoon some of our dancers met clandestinely to attend an underground "exhibition." The performance, which featured an exotic Parisian lovely and her lusty Arabian paramour, could be viewed only by invitation. You had to shell out—

in advance—approximately five times the cost of a ticket to the best seat at the ballet, plus swear on your mother's grave to keep your lip zipped. Several of the boys were approached by André Eglevsky, our featured male dancer, who had a "contact." Two of our guys bought in, but the viewing would be canceled without a larger audience, so invitations were extended more broadly. Melissa Hayden, one of the Company's star ballerinas, and Vida Brown, our eagle-eyed Ballet Mistress, boldly threw themselves into the breach. They coughed up twenty American dollars apiece and joined the little group of pilgrims who were so ardently seeking illumination.

Five of them gathered at a prearranged rendezvous with André's "contact" who hurried them to the rear of a small, dingy building. He sneaked them up a narrow wooden staircase to the first floor and escorted them into a darkish room furnished with several armchairs, a bed, and the two bare-naked performers. Our colleagues made themselves comfortable in the overstuffed chairs. They were studiously absorbing unusual angles in the art of the *pas de deux*, intent on esoteric new choreographic positions, when they heard sirens and clanging in the street below. Somebody shouted "Get out! Get out! The police!!" and *merde alors!* the party was over. They couldn't spill out of the place fast enough. One dancer threw open the first-floor window, flung himself out and raced back to his hotel, and his wife, at top speed. Turned out the police never came. Apparently, a prearranged shout of warning was the usual method of stopping the show and clearing the room when the performers got tired—or bored.

Paris had been cool and rainy, and while the Company was looking forward to a return engagement at the Champs Élysées in June, we were all glad to feel the warmth of the Tuscan sun. I was quartered with Barbara Walczak and Barbara Bocher on the Via Montebello, one street in from the river. The quiet little Pensione Pendini was equidistant from the Teatro Comunale on the one hand, shopping and major sightseeing points on the other. Plus, the landlady's unmarried son was not bad-looking. His English wasn't bad either and he operated real fast. In fact, before we'd completed our engagement, Mario Pendini had brilliantly proposed to each one of the three Barbaras as we all sat together atop Piazzale Michelangelo overlooking the city. He'd driven us across the river and up the hill one sunny afternoon to admire one of the great views of Florence. First he posed us at the foot of the bronze copy of the David and photographed his three American dancers. Then, turning to blond, blue-eyed Bocher (who could easily have stepped out of a Botticelli): "You are the prettiest," he announced. "And you are the sexiest," he informed me. "But you," he assured dark-haired, Polish-Catholic Walczak with great seriousness, "*you* are the one I would marry!" Fluffy white clouds floated over the city of the Medici—and of Machiavelli.

But we'd entered another war zone. For all its architectural beauty, for all the treasures it held, for all the history it had known, Florence had not escaped the war. In 1952, the only bridge left spanning the River Arno was the Ponte Vecchio. This, the city's oldest bridge, that almost holy site where young Dante first encountered the child Beatrice, alone had escaped the Allied bombing.

The Teatro Comunale, like the central train station, was modern in design and had been built recently. We rehearsed and performed in one of Mussolini's pet projects. The theater was not far from the river and within easy walking distance of the Piazza della Signoria where another replica of Michelangelo's David stood, this one in weather-stained marble. Close by was the Uffizi Gallery, where you could see Da Vincis and Botticellis and Giottos and astonishingly vivid twelfth-century triptychs. If you ventured outside the second floor onto a balcony at the far end of the hall, you could walk right around a sculptural grouping of the Laacoön, all tortured bodies and coiling snakes. In theory, we were supposed to save all our energy for dancing, but Mr. B never objected to our art-gallery excursions. On the contrary, he told us how the knowledgable Diaghilev had sent young Georgi Balanchivadze back again and again, and yet again, to study these very same works of art until, suddenly, something was revealed. The *quattrocento* and Renaissance paintings, so remote, so alien at first, now spoke to him directly. He had experienced a revelation, although he didn't use

Barbara Bocher and Barbara Walczak with Mario Pendini and two onlookers at Piazzale Michelangelo, Florence (1952). Author's collection.

Bocher, Milberg, and Walczak posing at base of statue of David, Piazzale Michelangelo (1952). Author's collection.

Walczak and Bocher with Mario Pendini, overlooking the city of Florence. Author's collection.

that word. "One day I saw them. I could really *see* them. I knew why he made me go back."

Backstage, the Comunale was a blessed change both from the Liceo and the older French theaters. The bathrooms were not quite so fragrant, and we changed in convenient, well-lit dressing rooms. On the top floor there was an enormous rectangular rehearsal hall, all mirrors and tall windows that looked out on the golden buildings and blue skies of Florence. Above our heads was a lofty ceiling draped in billowing white silk that was fastened at the corners and decorated in the center with a great crimson fleur-de-lys. The stage of the Comunale was springy and level, not raked, and there was a little backstage concession where you could get *pasta dolce* (pastries) and cappucino with powdered chocolate sprinkled on top from a little tin shaker.

That year, the following year, and for every European tour thereafter, the Company engaged the same three stagehands from the Comunale for our travels. The senior member was Oswaldo Costanzi: short, wiry, monkey-like, quick-witted. He was the boss. Then there was Walter Travagli: dark good looks, dependable, but not exactly a quiz kid. The third *macchinista* was fair-haired, blue-eyed, hollow-cheeked Lido, a.k.a. "Stromboli," who worked harder than anybody else but had a short fuse. Each time we arrived at a new city, Oswaldo would dispatch Lido to scout for a *trattoria* that served decent pasta while he and Walter set up backstage, thus diplomatically avoiding blow-ups with the local help. These *Fiorentini* considered themselves citizens of their region and their city rather than their country. When we played Rome the following year, they laughingly informed us that the "SPQR" (*Senatus PopulusQue Romanus*) carved on various stone monuments was not a Latin designation having to do with the Senate and populace of ancient Rome—but stood for *sono porci questi romani* ("they're all pigs, these Romans") in the vernacular. All three rode their bicycles between home and theater and, whenever they could borrow or cajole one from a friend or relative, a Vespa.

The powerful little motorbike (*vespa* means "wasp") was the Florentine's vehicle of choice. You could zoom around the city on

Bombed buildings, Florence (1952). The one bridge left spanning the
River Arno at that time was the Ponte Vecchio. Photo by author.

it with a friend perched in back, and it handled the Tuscan hill-
sides very nicely. For several members of the Company, including two of our principal dancers, Frank Moncion and Frank Hobi,
it was seduction on wheels. They practically salivated when they
saw one. Simon Sadoff, our pianist and second assistant conductor, succumbed.

Simon was a man of many gifts. He alternated with Kolya Kopeikine as accompanist for company classes and rehearsals. He
also possessed a resonant baritone, was an accomplished singer
of German *lieder*, and had an ear fine-tuned to the infinite quirks
and cadences of language. Unofficially, Simon was our human
joke-lexicon, a virtuoso in the sub-dialects of New York City and
South Jersey. His Yiddish accent was side-splitting: he could do ancient uncles, nerdy adolescents, and strictly orthodox *balabustahs*
(housewives). He could do Shanty-Irish, Harlem and Chinatown,
faithfully mimic a major league baseball player from Flatbush or a
minor Polish nobleman living in Astoria, and he possessed an un-
paralled command of Brooklynese and the grunting gangspeak of
"duh Brah-nex." He was uncanny. If we were homesick or feeling
the stress of constant language and currency change, we would beg
him—"Just once more, Simon!"—to parrot his favorite radio an-
nouncer on WNYC who delivered the "weddah reepawt" from "da
Bat'try" ("tempacha is toity-tuhree pernt tuhree"), or to expound on
anything in Simon's own regional patois, the exquisite refinements
of "Sout' Jaisey."

Simon succumbed to the call of the sporty little motorbike. So
did Frank Hobi. So did Mr. B. All three acquired brand-new Ves-
pas in Florence and had them crated to go in the Company's bag-
gage car. But they also conspired to break them out at least once
and ride like a trio of bandits alongside our train. Which is exactly
what they did.

We left the blue and gold city on the last day of May, performed
briefly in Lausanne and Zurich (where black swans paddled in the
river), then entrained for Paris and the Champs Élysées theater.
We were pretty relaxed this time. We'd been there, were familiar
with the theater, knew where to eat nearby, and how long it would

take to get to it from hotel or *pension*. Simon, on the other hand, was extremely jumpy. He was scheduled to conduct *Symphony in C* for the first time during this engagement—closely following guest conductor Pierre Monteux who, if I remember rightly, would direct the first performance. A celebrated conductor—and *French.* And to add another twist of the screw, this would be Simon's virgin ascent to the podium as Assistant Conductor for the company. This was not by any means his first venture at conducting ballet, but you could tell he was excited about it, wound up as tight as he could be. Doubtless, the Vespa was a welcome distraction.

Perhaps Mr. B was also keeping his mind off the return engagement. Our recent performances in Lausanne and Zurich may have dredged up unsettling memories: the onset of lung disease in Paris, the collapse of one of his lungs, the enforced rest and subsequent recovery in a Swiss tuberculosis sanatorium. Perhaps he was reminded of difficulties with his first wife, Tamara Geva, when they lived together in Paris. Or, just possibly, Mr. B was recalling how he'd scandalously sprung three Russian "baby ballerinas" on the Parisian dance public—Irina Baronova, age twelve, Tamara Toumanova, age thirteen, and Tatiana Riabouchinska, age fourteen—thus causing some anxiety to twenty-seven-year-old Alexandra Danilova who was currently living with him. These were all Paris scenarios.

For Balanchine, though, the past was past. You had the impression it was a memory region he considered dangerous, a sphere of overwhelming nostalgia, perhaps, where too long a backward look might prove paralyzing. The past could draw one in, swallow one up, suffocate one's powers under a blanket of melancholy, the Russian disease. He had seen his compatriots drawn in. Mr. B kept his focus on the present. "What's wrong with right now?" he would ask. On the other hand, while he rarely indulged in the delights or delusions of nostalgia, who can tell what he was thinking about, or trying not to think about, on the return to Paris?

Somewhere en route between Zurich and Paris, somebody hollered out "There they are!" It was almost too dark to see and the train was rattling along at a fast clip, but sure enough! There were those two lunatic *banditti*—Simon and Mr. B—not quite shoulder to shoulder, buzzing along on a road that ran parallel with the tracks, Frank following close behind. They waved, looking smug and happy and windblown all at once. They waved and we waved back and yelled "Hi! Hi!" to them, leaning way out the windows. Then the road separated from the train tracks and they were no more to be seen.

Not long after opening night, and shortly before Simon was to conduct *Symphony in C* for the very first time, word went round that Mr. B had composed a "limerick." At least, that's what he called it. The verses were in English, more or less, and Balanchine was clearly pleased with his modest venture into Anglo-Saxon poetics. With loving attention to metrics, he had fashioned alternating tetrameter/trimeter verses with an *a-b-a-b* rhyme scheme commemorating the Great Vespa Ride and, at the same time, celebrating Simon Sadoff's ascension to the podium. It wasn't too hard to get him to recite the piece. I may be wrong, but I think it was the day before Simon conducted, and I think Mr. B may have been just a little bit jealous. I should like to remark, in retrospect, that while it is extremely unlikely that Mr. Balanchine's verses could ever be mistaken for a true specimen of the classical limerick, they were worthy of a Don Quixote. Its syntax was brilliant—impeccably *Georgic*, if I may put it that way. The verses ran as follows (to be recited with gusto in a nasal Russian accent):

> Who likes to conduct big orchestra
> In Théâtre des Champs Élysées
> While I lubricating mine Vespa,
> And he Simonizing Bizet?

10

The Russian Easter Bribe

M R. B WASN'T the only one who made verses. All through that 1952 tour we composed ditties commemorating the stops along the way. "We" being myself and the other two Barbaras (Walczak and Bocher), along with Ruth Sobotka who was not only a gifted theatrical designer, but something of a Latin scholar, and the dancer who became film director Stanley Kubrick's second wife. Our savvy Vida Brown suggested popular songs and musical comedy numbers that might be turned to good use. "Barrr-celona! Where the wind comes sweeping down the drain!" we ripped from *Oklahoma*. To the nostalgic torch song, "The Last Time I Saw Paris," we added "was in the hotel john." We tried without much success to deliver the lyrics in the approved "chanteuse" style, husky and throaty. To the melody of "London Bridge Is Falling Down," we sang the Berlin song, each stanza ending with the refrain of "My big stomach!" — a no-no in any dance group but approaching mortal sin in Balanchine's company. Sung at a brisk pace, it went something like this:

> Ach! The Berlin food was great!
> So we ate, so we ate
> *Apfelkuchen* by the crate
> My big stomach!
> German men they were the rage
> Were the rage, were the rage,
> They all came back to see *The Cage*
> And my big stomach.

I think there was another stanza, then we switched to a languid Vienna waltz tempo for the conclusion:

> We are on our new diets still,
> Swallowing pill after reducing pill,
> Balanchivadze envisions with glee
> A ske-le-ton NYCB.

Along with sophomoric songs about Barcelona, Páris, and Berlin, we cranked out irreverent numbers satirizing our choreographers: Balanchine, Robbins, Bolender, and, later, Ruthanna Boris, Antony Tudor, and John Butler. Nobody was safe.

But there was more to it than adolescent high jinks. Our songs, if inelegant, were cathartic. Into these lyrics went the smelly bathrooms with ripped-up newspaper stuck on a hook for toilet paper, the dressing rooms lit by 40-watt bulbs, the blisters, the sprained ankles, the sore muscles, the splintery stages, the consignment of pointe shoes that never arrived, the backstage johnnies who thought "ballet dancer" equaled "call girl," the strange foreign foods, the diarrhea, and once or twice having to drag the body out of bed at 5 A.M. to catch a train after a late-night performance. The songs, the recognition and laughter they provoked, helped to put things in perspective. The hardships we'd experienced, the problems we'd come up against, were no longer "unsung."

Closing night is traditionally the time to play tricks on stage, a kind of anything-goes All Fools Night. Costumes were quietly stapled to the scenery; blacked-out teeth made for ghastly smiles; a couple of dancers were forced to move in unison when their *tutus* were safety-pinned together. Glue was omnipresent. Water pistols appeared. After five months of European travel, in 1952, we not only cut up on stage, but with little effort were persuaded to present a "Cabaret" of our tour songs at the closing night party. It would be a release. Everybody was in high spirits that night, not only from the drinks but giddy with the knowledge that we would actually be on our way home the next day. And everyone, including Mr. B, seemed to take our music-hall contribution to the party in good humor.

During the New York season after that five-month tour, we four in dressing room #7 (Sobotka, Kai, Walczak, Milberg) on the fourth floor of the City Center of Music and Drama continued to crank out parodies as the spirit moved us. And the spirit moved us greatly when we discovered that the select group of New York socialites who had formed a philanthropic organization called "Ballet Associates" were planning their annual dinner dance as a fundraiser for the company. Anatole Chujoy pointed out that "for the company this meant an additional few thousand dollars . . . and a certain recognition by social circles that had thus far neglected the company."[1] When we learned that the upcoming festivity was to take place in the Grand Ballroom of the Waldorf Astoria, dressing room #7 immediately set about composing appropriate stanzas to celebrate the stately event. These occasional verses were not set to music; they were packed with lewd double-entendres; and I have no idea how Mr. Balanchine learned about them.

The Ballet Ball was set for November 28, 1952. Over six hundred guests were reported by *Dance News* in the January 1953 issue. The list ranged from Old New York money to theatrical celebrities, and included a prince, a count, a Monseigneur of the Church, poet Edith Sitwell, designer Cecil Beaton, and television comedienne Imogene Coca, along with principal dancers from the Ballet Russe, Ballet Theatre, and our own NYCB. Tanaquil, who would marry Mr. Balanchine that New Year's Eve, was photographed wearing an insouciant party-hat tied under her chin with ribbons. Maria Tallchief, recently divorced from Mr. B, sat at another table with her new husband, the dashing Elmourza Natirboff, a professional pilot who (so we heard) raced his D-Jaguar between flights. There was J. Alden Talbot without whom (according to *Dance News*) "the annual ball would not take place." There was Mrs. Alice Pleydell-Bouverie, the Chairperson of the Committee—and of course there were Mr. and Mrs. Lincoln Kirstein. Mrs. Kirstein, née Fidelma Cadmus, was the sister of Paul Cadmus, the painter, and an artist in her own right. An imposing figure, with pale skin and severely coiled dark hair, she dressed with ascetic spareness and wore a large cross as her only ornament. The guest list was diversified and impressive and the Ballet Associates Ball may well have been the event of the season. Dressing room #7 had not received invitations.

It was obvious to anyone connected with the company that Lincoln Kirstein and George Balanchine had joined forces for a common purpose, to form a ballet company that could rival any in Europe. It was equally clear that their agendas were not always parallel. Balanchine was primarily focused on creating interesting new works and committed to developing dancers—significantly, female dancers—who could handle his choreographic intricacies with intelligence and grace. His sources of inspiration and invention were invariably women. "In ballet (sniff, sniff)," he would patiently explain to some poor guy who had mishandled his partner, "woman is *queen*." This was not the case with Lincoln.

Lincoln Kirstein was a Harvard graduate, a *litterateur*, a published poet and critic, the founder of *Hound and Horn* (a respected literary periodical) and of the scholarly *Dance Index*, to which he was a major contributor. It seems that he was heir to a sizeable chunk of Filene's Department Store. I don't ever recall him sitting down. I can still see him in his navy peajacket at the School, a huge figure with jutting jaw and clean-shaven scalp, standing in the doorway intently watching ballet class. Ann Inglis told me years later that Lincoln reminded her of the statues on Easter Island when he stood in the doorway, granite-faced, without motion or expression. Despite his marriage he was sexually attracted to men, and primarily interested in the company's male dancers. He was deeply engaged not only with dance but with painters, ar-

chitects, museum curators, and composers such as Gian Carlo
Menotti and Virgil Thomson, with whom he maintained close relations. Lincoln was a polymath, as someone once pointed out, and
a figure to be reckoned with; a powerful mover within the modernist enterprise. As might be expected, he knew who was on the cut-
ting edge, who might be persuaded to contribute generously to the
arts, and with whom he cared to associate. He was not unkind but,
to put it crudely, he was a snob. An enlightened energetic enthusiastic snob. And Mr. B, while something of an elitist himself, was
not invariably in harmony with Lincoln's myriad projects.

Who told Mr. B about our masterpiece? In any case, he found
out. He wanted to hear the poem we'd composed about the Ballet
Ball; he *really* would like to hear it; just once; wouldn't we say it for
him privately? he would tell no one, absolutely no one. In short, he
hounded us mercilessly. I told Mr. B straight out we couldn't *possibly* recite it to him, or to anybody. It was just a silly set of rhymes—
and it was too dirty to say out loud. Period. Of course this had
the reverse effect. He ceased his importuning and *ordered* Barbara
Walczak and me, very sweetly, to give up the rhymes. He had a
plan. We would go into the freight elevator that serviced the backstage, just the three of us. It had thick quilted padding, old and
frayed but soundproof. Nobody would overhear. And that, he cunningly promised, would be the end of it.

So Basia and I marched into the elevator with Mr. Balanchine,
stopped it between the second and third floors, and repeated the
dreadful ditty. All three stanzas. I could feel my face flushing with
embarrassment and suppressed giggles. Eyes shining, Mr. B now
proposed a diabolical exchange. If the three Barbaras agreed to
sing a selection of our tour songs—*and* recite these verses—at
the Ballet Associates Dinner Dance, he would ask Simon Sadoff to
accompany us and he, Balanchine, would personally introduce us.
We would be *his* invited guests. We started to shake our heads. *And*
we would all be invited to his Russian Easter feast in April! That he
prepared with his own hands.

Balanchine personally introduced "The Three Barbaras" and then turned the mike over to us. As arranged, Simon accompanied two or three tour songs. Each one received a polite scatter of applause. But, as we prepared to recite the loaded verses Simon sneaked ostentatiously off the platform. I mean, he made it crystal clear that he would have no affiliation with what came next. He would not sit quietly at the piano. He would have no part in it. My heart quailed. But the moment had come, and there was tacit agreement among us to put the best possible face on it. So we pulled ourselves bravely upright, took a deep breath, and in upbeat lighthearted cadence we chanted:

> Oh it's balls that keep us in business,
> Like this Ballet Ball of the year;
> If it weren't for successful balls
> None of us would be here!

It went on like that, leading to a conclusion at the end of the second stanza that "Two balls are better than one," which led directly to the third and final stanza's *dénoument*, the inescapable proposition that "Three balls are better than two."

This poetic effort dropped into a profound silence, a vacuum made more hollow by the few faint claps that petered out almost before they could be heard. In the moment or two before we fled the platform, I saw the stone faces of the assembled guests. They showed a total absence of expression. An eloquent blankness. A roaring non-response. The one response possible to *gentillesse* in the presence of *crudità*.

April rolled around and Mr. B paid his debt. We gorged on rich homemade *pascha* and *kulitch*, the traditional Russian Easter cakes, at the Balanchines' apartment on East 74th Street. A few blocks east, on Second Avenue, stood the Greek Orthodox Holy Trinity Cathedral, which lent an added sanctity to the occasion, especially when I learned that there would be a candlelight procession around the church at midnight. We were introduced to other guests, and after several false alarms during which Mr. B went to look down the stairwell, to a latecomer he kept promising would be his "little surprise." The "little surprise" turned out to be Hershy Kay, composer and orchestrator, who made Stravinsky look tall. Hershy would be arranging the music for *Western Symphony*, scheduled for the following year. The two other Barbaras appeared to be at ease and enjoying themselves, but in spite of the genuine hospitality I was uncomfortably aware of a kind of irony surrounding the proceedings. I couldn't help considering the unholy nature of the "litany" that had gained me entrance to the Easter Feast— and the shameless bribe that had lured me there.

Lincoln never reproved us for the scandalous verses. In fact, I don't recall that Mr. Kirstein noticed our existence for a long time after the fiasco in the Ballroom. I couldn't help wondering, though, just what had motivated Mr. B. What demon possessed him? Had he capitulated to a lurking anti-snob activism? Or to his mischievous Tyl Eulenspiegel streak? Maybe he just wanted to show off his girls. But, looking back, I believe he'd hit on an irresistible way to irritate Lincoln.

Roy Tobias and Barbara Milberg between tours, at Miami Beach, Florida (1951). Author's collection.

Nicky Magallanes and Milberg, Miami Beach. Author's collection.

Milberg and Tobias, Miami Beach. Author's collection.

II

Opus 34 and the Loopies

$\mathcal{I}$N JANUARY, for the 1954 New York season, we presented a weird ballet set to Arnold Schoenberg's twelve-tone movie score, *Opus 34*. It was the first of four new Balanchine ballets we premiered that year. These were major works and the list was staggering, to put it mildly: *Nutcracker* followed the Schoenberg almost immediately in February; *Western Symphony* and *Ivesiana* premiered a week apart the following September. In addition, between our mid-winter and fall seasons, Mr. B was setting the dances for *House of Flowers*, a musical comedy featuring Geoffrey Holder and a cast of black and Caribbean singers and dancers—one of whom was young Arthur Mitchell who would soon join the company. Not one of these productions was remotely like *Opus 34*.

The Schoenberg was danced in four sections deliberately entitled to suggest the progress of a disaster: "Threat," "Danger," "Fear," and "Catastrophe." But the music was structured in two equal parts, not four. Balanchine had split the ballet right down the middle by dividing the music into a "First Time" and a "Second

Time." That is, the score was played once and then repeated from beginning to end. Two identical sections, neither of them very pretty.

The choreography departed radically from the style of movement Mr. B had devised for Hindemith's *Four Temperaments*, eight years earlier. Hindemith and Schoenberg both were German composers and both wrote contemporary music. But *Four Ts* had melodies you could whistle or hum—or sing (*"dah-DAH-de-da-DAH"*) when you taught a new girl the entrance steps in the "Melancholic" variation. The score had moments of humor, whimsy, surprise, all of which were neatly reflected in the dances. And you knew exactly where you were at any point in the section you were dancing; the rhythmic impulses were clear, precise, easy to count. Not so the Schoenberg.

Did Balanchine conceive the physical movement of *Opus 34* as a reflection—or possibly a rejection?—of the seemingly a-rhythmic, unmelodious, arcane intricacies of twelve-tonal music? The score ranged in mood from the ominous to the strident to the shocking. It whined and gloomed and muttered and crashed, and you could never be sure you'd counted it accurately. You could be sure, however, that Mr. B had selected this particular music with his usual care. He'd chosen to experiment with a score originally composed for a movie—and in truth, the spirit of *Opus 34* seemed closer to a science-fiction horror film or *The Return of the Mummy* or *The Night of the Living Dead* or to *Nosferatu*, the German vampire classic, than to his earlier flirtation in *Four Ts* with German Expressionism, polyphony, and medieval alchemy. And there was another thing to wonder about: Had Mr. B folded some message into the doubling of the score? A suggestion of "two-timing" built into the two "times" of the ballet?

Choreography by George Balanchine vividly describes the divided sections of *Opus 34*: "The FIRST TIME is performed in an extreme vocabulary of dance motion. The SECOND TIME is an endurance of horror, a grisly symbolic surgery in pantomime, with dancers costumed in bandages and as cadavers."[1] Edwin Denby, dean of dance reviewers, noted the ballet's "darkly glistening and oppressive" score, the "sounds of it, the whirrs, squeals, reverberations, hums and thuds," but cast a more positive light over the strange happenings on stage. "It is a powerful and it is a paradoxical ballet," he wrote. In the first part, "you watch the compressed phrases, the reversals, the intricate developments. . . . In the second part, the music floods out like a soundtrack, weird as a spell of science fiction, inexorable in the timing of its dreadful stream. The audience," he noted, "watches the first part absorbed and impressed; it watches the second fascinated, frightened and giggling. Then the curtain comes down and there is a curious vacuum."[2] I dimly recall Tanaquil in a white or light gray body suit being manipulated by two men, held over a hospital cart and turned almost inside-out, "operated on" in midair with those elegant legs forced open, her behind spread out toward the audience. It was obscene and appalling.

I was in *Opus 34*, whether as bandaged corpse or naked cadaver I do not (as Borges might say) choose to remember. But I remember very clearly that during our February-March season the following year, I became a bona fide casualty, my right leg in a cast to the knee. I'd landed in one of the City Opera's scary little scenery holes during an entrance in *Swan Lake*. When I regained consciousness, I crawled offstage on all fours with little winged swans hopping past me in both directions. Along with the rapidly swelling sprained ankle, an x-ray revealed a cracked fifth metatarsal bone, a hairline fracture. That was not the worst of it. It looked like that one stupid misstep was going to keep me from traveling, in April, on our 1955 European tour. Three months in France, Italy, Portugal, Switzerland, and Germany. Most devastating of all, the company would open in Monaco at the Grand Théâtre du Casino de Monte Carlo. The Côte d'Azur, the gaming tables, the famous gardens, a bachelor Prince!! Romantic, fabled Monte Carlo, where Kolya Kopeikine had first met Mr. Balanchine. How I yearned to go! My plaster cast itched like the very devil and the doctor had predicted a minimum of six weeks in it. I scratched inside with a chopstick, clumped around, and lusted after April in Monte Carlo.

Mr. B took pity on me. *If* the fracture were healed sufficiently to have the cast removed by the time we left, the company would take me along. I would not have to dance in Monte Carlo but could start with an easy ballet in Marseilles, the next stop. I had the damned thing off in three weeks and spent the enforced holiday catching up on my favorite reading. *Star Science Fiction Stories* had ten brand new tales. There were stories by Asimov and Bradbury, Arthur Clarke and Philip K. Dick. And there was a really spooky one called "Dance of the Dead" by Richard Matheson, a writer I hadn't encountered before. It was a kind of pop/horror vision of the not-too-distant future that thrilled and chilled me—and reminded me of *Opus 34.*

I told the plot to Mr. Balanchine and Leon Barzin, the company's primary conductor, on the plane to France. Barzin was a fine musician and a vigorous conductor who led the orchestra with mathematical precision and Mediterranean passion. Most of the time he kept his energies under control, but occasionally he couldn't resist setting the *tempi* a bit too fast and forcing the dancers, especially the principal dancers, to speed up like an old newsreel. Leon's second wife and, he later admitted, his first consuming love, was tall and slender, a classical beauty. She looked rather like a fair-haired Virginia Woolf. The daughter of a diplomat, Eleanor Post Barzin had inherited from her mother a chateau at Vaux sur Seine, complete with Arcadian woods, formal gardens, ponds, a grotto, follies, statuary, and a small but well-appointed private theater. One unforgettable day-and-night-off when we were dancing in Paris, Eleanor and Leon entertained the entire company there.

Midway through the long flight over the Atlantic, I found Barzin and Balanchine sitting together in the downstairs lounge of our BOAC Stratocruiser, quietly drinking coffee. In my innocence, I had the idea that Mr. B might like to cap the Schoenberg with an even spookier "nightmare ballet" (as Bernard Taper called it), a science fiction ballet this time, using the Richard Matheson scenario. Truly, it is said, fools stomp in where angels fear to lightly tread. But Balanchine was willing to listen and Barzin didn't object, so I launched in enthusiastically: "It's called 'Dance of the Dead.' Really *really* scary. There's this bunch of college kids in a probability world, maybe the future," I chirp. "They're driving too fast and drinking and getting high on some drug and singing 'Olive Oyl, you is my goil' and they're going to a nightclub they're not supposed to. This is where it gets weird, like *Opus 34*."

Mr. B listens politely; Leon's expression registers disapproval. "They're gonna see these 'loopies' dance in a kind of prize ring," I continue with more gravity. "See, they're really dead people, corpses, who've been injected with a serum, a virus that makes them jerk around." Mr. B is beginning to look interested. Mr. Barzin is growing distinctly irritated. "That's what they do for entertainment," I amplify, "watch these 'loopies'—it stands for *Lifeless Undead Phenomenon*, LUP—until one of the dead dancers jerks over the ropes and falls onto one of the college kids. . . ."

Here Leon cuts in. He can't take any more. Why am I wasting my time on this trash? he wants to know. Why don't I read some *good* literature, something that will develop my mind? He turns to Mr. B: "She should be reading classics, George." Suddenly I'm freezing. Now Balanchine becomes the peremptory one, although he does not raise his voice: "She can read *any* thing she likes!" I melt. Leon casts his indignant, extremely well-educated black eyes to the spot on the ceiling where the Olympians hover, while Mr. Balanchine assures me the story was very interesting—here he pats me on the shoulder—and I should just go on reading *any*thing I want, as long as it gives me pleasure. I took his advice.

In Monte Carlo as the ankle healed and the bone knit together, I began to stretch and do simple exercises at the barre, preparing with some anxiety to dance an "easy ballet" in Marseilles. In the evenings, though, while my compatriots were performing before (a pre-Grace Kelly) Prince Rainier who actually appeared in the Royal Box, I sneaked into the Casino where employees of the Principality are strictly forbidden to gamble. Once or twice I bumped into Kolya Kopeikine who was silently floating toward the baccarat table. I played roulette with the beautiful pearly chips marked *Ste des Bains de Mer,* MONACO, and collected modest winnings for myself and for everybody who slipped me francs to bet for them. Kolya, clearly an old hand at these very gaming tables, didn't do so well. He muttered to whoever would listen that the *mistral* was blowing, such an ill wind that brought *terrible* bad luck.

I was very naturally grateful that Mr. Balanchine allowed me to go on tour with the company, but I couldn't have been more astonished to find him defending my right to read "pulp fiction" in the face of Leon's onslaught. I don't think he particularly wanted to do another horror ballet. Or another Schoenberg. He'd slain the twelve-tone dragon and was headed due West, toward American rhythms and American folkways.

12

Mr B Gets Mad

*J*UST EIGHT MONTHS after the first performance of *Opus 34*, we premiered *Western Symphony* and *Ivesiana* within a week of each other. *Western Symphony* was brilliantly orchestrated by Hershy Kay (the "little surprise" at the Russian Easter feast); its themes included such old-time favorites as "Good Night, Ladies," "Oh, Dem Golden Slippers," and "The Girl I Left Behind Me." Tanny, wearing a broad-brimmed hat with curling feathers, brought the house down in the fourth movement with her flirtatious, cocky, dance-hall bravado. And *Ivesiana*, set to several of Charles Ives's chamber pieces, had sections with titles like "Central Park in the Dark," "Barn Dance," and "Hallowe'en." Each in its own way was genuine "Americana."

In Ives, Balanchine had found a contemporary American composer, a virtually unknown New Englander, whose music ranged from polyphony to ragtime, from choirs to folk music, from sonatas to hymns to popular songs. This was quintessentially "native music," but closer to Scott Joplin (at times, closer to Schoenberg) than to the arrangements of Virgil Thomson or Aaron Copland. In 1939, when Ives's *Second Sonata for Piano* was performed at Town Hall in New York, Lawrence Gilman, the music critic for the *Herald Tribune* wrote that it was "the greatest music composed by an American, and the most deeply and essentially American in impulse and implication."[1]

When Balanchine began to work on *Ivesiana*, in 1954, the composer had just died at the age of eighty. But he was clearly a kindred spirit; his experiments as broad in scope, as varied, as extreme as Balanchine's own. It may be that Charles Ives's embrace of the immense variety of music surrounding him led Balanchine to explore other labyrinths than those introduced by twelve-tone systems. For that September season yielded up not only the local rituals, urban mysteries, and philosophical conundrums of *Ivesiana*, but the supercharged dance-hall music, the cowboy laments, the folk tunes and heart-wrenching spirituals that he and Hershy had chosen for *Western Symphony*. For those of us in *Ivesiana*, though, a rehearsal of that ballet very briefly opened a window onto a Balanchine I had never seen before and would never see again. It was during the final stage rehearsal of Ives that the dancers of the New York City Ballet heard our stoic, level-headed choreographer lose his temper.

Ivesiana premiered on September 14, 1954, with two conductors. Conducting at the same time. Hugo Fiorato, our first violinist and the first assistant conductor, led the string section and Leon directed the rest of the orchestra. Looking down from the stage, you could see them both together on the podium, Hugo canted to the right and Barzin with his back to him, facing the winds and brass and percussion. Hugo made graceful sweeps with his baton; Leon's strokes were scaled down to precise verticals and horizontals, as if confined within a box, and pointed stabs toward various instruments. Sometimes their movements were synchronized; sometimes both were conducting but not at the same tempo; at times, only one would be galvanized in a sudden spurt. It looked like an old Charlie Chaplin film, a jerky black-and-white "silent" with unexpectedly discordant accompaniment. As for picking up cues, you were never quite sure which conductor to follow.

Balanchine had designed a section of Ives, *The Unanswered Question*, for Todd Bolender, the young Allegra Kent, and four boys who would turn, twist, manipulate, and move the slender girl through space. This was Allegra's first major role, and I knew it was one of Mr. Balanchine's "I give myself a challenge" essays in movement. Not long before, coming down the stairs from the wardrobe room, I'd caught up with our choreographer on the landing between the first and second floors and brashly taken the opportunity to inquire about something I'd been curious about for a long time: "Can I ask you a question, Mr. B? How do you make up all those new steps?" Continuing down the stairs he responded airily (impatient, I think, hindered from going to wherever he was headed). "W-a-a-l . . . [sniff] . . . it's like making salad, you know? Just mix up same old vegetables a little different," he answers blithely, "maybe little tomato this time, throw in some mushroom. . . ." I break into the recital of salad ingredients. No, that's not what I mean, I pursue. At the landing nearest to the stage he stops, looks at me quizzically. What did I want to know? So I tell him I want to know how he invents steps, movements that have never been done before, ever, anywhere. Like those wonderful lifts in *Barocco*, I explain, where the man has both hands on his partner's waist and she helps by grasping his wrists and pushing up from them. Nobody ever did that lift before, I say, and now everyone's using it. How did you do that? Now he looks hard at me. Silence. "I give myself chal-lenge" he answers slowly, "like *Orpheus* pas de deux. She wants him to look at her; he must not. *Metamorphoses*," he goes on, "girl *always* on pointe, boy *never* stand up. Challenge." I nod understanding, and he disappears through the door to the stage.

The challenge presented in *The Unanswered Question* was similar to the one in *Orpheus*, but far more complex. In *Orpheus* the partners must dance close together, the man with his head averted and the woman coaxing him to look at her. The tension is parallel,

Stage rehearsal of *Ivesiana* (1954). Allegra Kent, supported by Jonathan Watts (in white), Gene Gavin (center), Gerald Leavitt (in black), and Brooks Jackson (behind). Mr. B stands at left; Todd Bolender relaxes on floor. Photograph by Radford Bascome, courtesy of Allegra Kent, from the estate of Joseph Cornell.

Hugo Fiorato, conductor, and Mr. B indulging in a bit of clowning back-stage before a performance of *Metamorphoses* (1952). Photographer unknown, author's collection.

so to speak, and the movement logical to those familiar with the story. In *Ivesiana*, the situation is reversed. She, like some vision of the holy grail, floats above, radiant in the spotlight; he, crawling along the floor, reaches up from the dark, tries to touch her, grasp her, but never quite manages to do so. To add to the complications, the four boys must partner and lift Allegra with one mind, as it were, operate with the inevitability of a closed system. Dressed entirely in black, they seem to disappear into and reappear from the surrounding darkness. She—loose golden hair, bare legs, simple white leotard, unattainable—is manipulated by invisible forces. Cloaked by the darkness on stage and their own black covering, accompanied by long drawn out, always changing chords as from an organ, the boys transport her through space. They turn her every way, up and down, on end, bring her within inches of the reaching hand; then lifting the illuminated being higher and higher, slowly withdraw into a rear wing like a star disappearing into the night. The segment was unforgettable: mysterious, hallucinatory, a dream-allegory.

For some reason, Mr. B was strung out at the orchestra rehearsal. There was never enough money to rehearse the musicians to the satisfaction of all concerned, and the music for this ballet was not simple. Plus, the budget required us to combine the orchestra rehearsal with the go-through for lighting. These were traditionally kept separate, and for good reasons. While orchestra rehearsal was almost always a stop-and-start session, you probably danced "full out" once or twice to get used to the tempi. Stage lighting was a slow, boring business for the dancers; you stood around in costume on assigned spots, for millennia it seemed, while the lighting director and stage manager and choreographer and maybe Lincoln Kirstein whispered together in the house. Then the lights were set up, changed, changed back, and rearranged as you "walked through" the steps again and again. It was unnerving to do both orchestra and lighting at once, especially so close to the opening.

But there was more to it than the lack of money and the chaos of combined rehearsals. Balanchine was launching a new star at the New York audience, and *The Unanswered Question* was tricky business. All kinds of things could go wrong. During a five-minute break, Dunya, the Ghengis Khan of the Wardrobe, had come downstairs with flashing eyes to scold Mr. B for making dancers crawl on the floor in this ballet. (Todd wore black, and so did the four boys, but the dancers in other sections did not.) You could hear her outraged protests in the hall. How could she take care of dirty cos-toom? Have to clean every time dance! Ballet dancers not supposed to crawl on floor!! Nobody had ever seen her in such a state. Or heard her howl at Mr. Balanchine. He managed to quiet the distraught wardrobe mistress, speaking in Russian. I wondered though, after he exploded, what else or who else he'd had to handle that day.

The section we broke up over was *In the Night*, the concluding section of the ballet, the very one that had so incensed Dunya. We'd stood around all afternoon while they fine-tuned the lighting; stopped and started while the two-headed orchestra repeated difficult passages. By this time I was tired, bored out of my mind, and growing skittish. As it turned out, quite a few of us were in much the same condition when, at long last, Mr. B called out for us to get in place for the closing section.

In the Night opens on an empty stage with corps members moving out randomly from the wings—on their knees. Boys and girls emerge at random intervals from all three downstage wings on both sides of the stage, as I recall, moving slowly and awkwardly toward center, drawing closer and closer to one another. The only things in motion are thighs; arms are held close at your sides; eyes look straight ahead. What you could see peripherally on either side, and frontally, coming directly at you, were half figures, bodies cut off at the knee. Dwarfish abnormal shapes. I saw fair-haired, blue-eyed Brooks Jackson, one of the taller boys, strolling toward me on his knees. This was a far cry from the "drag show" that Brooks and Shaun O'Brien and a couple of the other boys had put on between rehearsals a few days before.

I'd got back early from lunch, taken my coffee into the house, and joined the others who were resting there and watching our boys "camp." A stand with a single caged bulb was lighting the stage. First Brooksie (a.k.a. "Emma") jammed his feet, thick socks, ballet slippers and all, into a couple of empty coffee containers, rose shakily on pointe, and began to *pas de bourrée* around the stage, arms hung out, head drooping—a cast-off Giselle. Shaun, not to be outdone, also assumed coffee-container pointe shoes and flung himself passionately into the Swan Queen's solo variation, with much regal preening of feathers and flapping of wings. This inevitably segued into *The Dying Swan* whereupon Shaun/ Pavlova expired on the stage floor, his body bent double over one extended leg, arms crossed at the wrist, fingers fluttering weakly. The third—Bruce? Billy? Gerry Leavitt?—grabbed his towel and, using it for a scarf, plunged wildly about the stage à la Isadora Duncan, until somebody loudly called for "walkin' music." To the rhythmic clapping of the rest of us who were sprawled around the orchestra, the guys launched one after the other into a Gypsy Rose Lee routine, each one steamier than the one before, lewd bumps and grinds and the teasing removal of layer upon layer of clothing—doubly amazing because the only skin actually bared by any of the "strippers" was a single coy shoulder.

Now, after a mind-numbing rehearsal, the City Center stage was populated by paraplegic figures, rigid torsos moving slowly toward stage center on their knees. At this point, most unfortunately, someone whispered *"Toulouse-Lautrec!"* It was distinct enough to be heard all over the stage. Instantly, every moving torso looked like the little painter of the *Moulin Rouge*, sketcher of laughing ladies with questionable reputations—that gifted unhappy aristocrat with a trunk of normal size and disproportionately short legs—wearing a black dome of a hat. It was not fair.

I saw Brooksie approaching me. *The little painter raised from the dead.* How can I explain? Brooks was gazing straight at me, his expression bland but *knowing*, and he had a wicked gleam in his eye. I tried to look past him; I tried, desperately, not to see him, or look at anybody. I held it in as long as was humanly possible but the next time I raised my eyes from the floor and saw yet *another* Toulouse-Lautrec heading my way, I let out a loud snort. Couldn't help it. I focused on the floor again but heard a suppressed giggle on my left. Then another. Someone's shoulders were quivering. Somebody choked. Then the dam burst and we were laughing, howling, shrieking, gasping. It was unbearable. I flipped over on my back and did a "dead bug," fists curled in the air, knees bent, feet stuck out—a leftover antic from Jerry Robbins's insect ballet, *The Cage.* One or two others followed suit. That tore it.

Balanchine rose from his seat in the empty house, stormed onto the stage and gave it to us. We could go join ROCKETTES!! We could audition for Radio City Music Hall—four shows a *day*, every day same show!—*no* union. Maybe we like it better there? Maybe we do better with Rockettes, pay attention!? *Plenty* dancers want to be in New York City Ballet, *plenty* replacement! If we want to dance with New York City Ballet, no more nonsense! We do *In the*

Night from beginning, *NOW*. No more laughing, no more nonsense! He was really mad. Chastened, we scurried into the wings and managed to get through the last section of *Ivesiana* with becoming sobriety.

Maybe it was purely accidental, but looking back it seems to me there was a telling connection between Allegra's appearance in *Ivesiana* and Tanny's horrid "operation" in *Opus 34*. The Schoenberg had preceded the Ives by eight months. Each of them showed a completely passive female being intricately manipulated by faceless movers, but while the one was negative and repellant, the other was uplifting and alive—a positive breathing reversal of the first. One seemed unholy, the other a sacred mystery. In these contrasting modes, whether it was deliberate, intuitive, or accidental, Balanchine had fashioned a bridge from the undead to the living, from rigor and limitation to flexible possibility, from physical mortality to immortal Idea.

13

Of Rats and Mice and Candy-Canes

ETWEEN THE TWO avant-garde experiments set to contemporary music in 1954, Balanchine had taken the time
to stage a traditional, elaborate, evening-long spectacle. *The Nutcracker* was old-fashioned and romantic, its Tchaikovsky themes familiar to every music-lover and ballet-goer. The setting for the first
act was a family Christmas with lots of children; the second act
presented a series of divertissements, a Grand Pas de Deux, and a
sparkling Dewdrop surrounded by waltzing pink roses. There was
a walnut-shell boat and a child's dreamscape where everything was
made of candy. The production was truly spectacular, hugely popular—a success.

Season after season we'd presented ballets in simple tunics, set
against a bare cyclorama. Rarely was there a budget for scenery or
costumes. Madame Karinska sometimes contributed costumes to
the Company free of charge, especially when her establishment

had realized a substantial profit from *The Ice-Capades*. When we did the Hindemith *Metamorphoses*, in 1952, there was absolutely no money for scene designers or scenery. Jean Rosenthal, our lighting director, went to some mattress factory or outlet and came back with a couple of hundred bedsprings of various sizes. She put the stage crew to work gilding them, artfully connected them and hung them like Calder mobiles from the flies. It was a fabulous solution. It joined the backstage stock of legends.

Nutcracker had a strictly limited budget, but it boasted a Christmas Tree that grew and grew, aglitter with tiny lights, until it rose past the proscenium arch and filled the stage. It had an enchanted little white bed that glided about by itself; it had a snowstorm. Among other effects, there were forty Episcopal voices from the Boys Choir of nearby St. Thomas's, angelically accompanying scene changes. The first act featured a spooky old Toymaker named Herr Drosselmayer (a character part performed by Mischa Arshansky, actor and make-up artist, a role once or twice played by a heavily made-up Mr. B himself), and a fierce battle between hordes of mice and battalions of toy soldiers—the whole drawn from E. T. A. Hoffman's early nineteenth-century tale, "The Nutcracker and the Mouse King."

Nutcracker was both a throwback and a recovery. It sprang from full-scale productions of the work at the Maryinsky Theater in the St. Petersburg of Balanchine's boyhood, and it was his special gift to the children of the City of New York. As a student, young Georgi had performed the role of the Nutcracker who transforms into a Little Prince; later he'd played the terrifying Mouse King. When he became a full-fledged member of the Maryinsky Company he performed the hoop dance, the difficult solo variation to the music of the "Trepak," in which, according to contemporary witnesses, he distinguished himself. In later productions, including the Ballet Russe production familiar to New Yorkers (something closer to "highlights" from *Nutcracker*) that tasking variation was dropped and the "Trepak" split into the dance of the "Three Ivans"—a spirited competition among three boastful peasant lads.

Mr. Balanchine restored the original candy-cane hoop dance as a divertissement for Robert Barnett—who possessed the vitality and endurance of all three Ivans in one compact physique—and six little candy-cane girls who manipulated six little hoops. According to Barnett, when he was learning the steps Mr. B told Bobby that this was the one part he, Balanchine, had coveted ever since he was a little boy. (Significantly, apart from mimed passages, it is the only dance in the whole of Balanchine's *Nutcracker* that survives intact with its original Petipa-Ivanov choreography.) Balanchine set the hoop dance for Bobby just as it had been passed down to him, step for step. Bobby had chronic trouble with his left knee, an old injury from his high school days, but you'd never know it to see him in *Nutcracker*. What a jump he had! In his red-and-white striped costume, Bobby expertly leapt in and out and over his hoop as he whirled and twirled at 200 rpm—a peppermint candy-cane spinning as dizzily as a top. A visible explosion of energy. Wild applause every time, especially from the kids in the audience.

At the Maryinsky, according to Mr. B, German engineers were employed to create the stage effects for Imperial productions. They were permanent members of the staff and incredibly clever, Balanchine said, with mechanical apparatus. In *Swan Lake* and *The Nutcracker*, objects were made to move without visible agency, like our own little white bed. In the Maryinsky's five-act *Swan Lake*, wooden swans slid across the stage like real swans over water. Mr. B described how these engineers had made vines grow up columns in *La Belle au Bois Dormant* ("Sleeping Beauty") to show the passage of time, and how they'd invented machinery that enabled dancers to fly across the stage on unseen wires.

So far as I know, Balanchine attempted to reproduce the "flying on wires" effect only once, in his first setting of the Orpheus myth to Gluck's *Orfeo ed Euridice* at the old Metropolitan Opera House. In this short-lived production designed by Pavel Tchelitchev, Hades was updated to "a concentration camp with flying military slave-drivers lashing forced labor."[1] Choreographer Ruthanna Boris, then one of the young dancers in the opera, recalls how the slave-driver Furies "carried hatchets and made horrible grimaces" and added that they might have had "traffic problems."[2] This may be

Bobby Barnett, executing the Hoop Dance in *Nutcracker* (1955). Photographer unknown, courtesy Robert Barnett.

pure hearsay, but I'd been told that the Furies-on-wires actually banged into each other during the first performance. In any case the audience hated it. The critics reviled it. After the second performance, it was never seen again.

Nobody was "wired" in *The Nutcracker* except maybe the kids in the cast. The children, students chosen from the School, were almost electrically attentive, while Mr. B treated them with the grave courtesy he reserved for the very young. At dress rehearsal, I noticed him going over the pantomime passage in Act II with our pink-satin-clad Little Prince, collegially showing him a bow, a formal gesture, motions he himself had been taught. Balanchine was particularly good, though, at demonstrating to the Mice Squadron how to be "nice mice." He hunched his back and curled his hands up at chin level, fingers playing an invisible keyboard, eyes agleam, shifting in their sockets, a devilish expression dawning on his face. Then, nose twitching, he darted hither and thither in short spurts. It was almost too graphic.

Several of us commented on his brilliant rodent-act during a break. He grew thoughtful. "Yes, I am like rat." The staging of this ballet had obviously brought back a flood of memories, none very pleasant. He began to describe what it was like to live in St. Petersburg directly after the 1917 Revolution. I, for one, had never heard him go into detail about this period before. The students were starving, he said. Everybody was starving; nobody had enough food. There were soldiers everywhere; people begging, sorting through garbage. The Maryinsky was closed, the Imperial Ballet School was finished, shut down. No classes. No teachers. No meals. Nobody to tell them how to survive. It was dangerous in the streets. "I was hungry *all the time*. I was youngest boy with group of boys from School." Georgi tagged along behind the older boys. "We stay together, safer." Sometimes, he went on, after a pause during which you sensed the memory was growing vivid, "sometimes we go down in basement of theater, very dark. Can't sleep. We hunt rats. Sometimes we find. Plenty rats down there."

"Why were you looking for rats?" we asked.

"To eat. I was scared like hell but I was hungry, starving. Long time we have no food. Sometimes we catch rat and we kill and we eat."

He was thirteen years old.

In her memoir, Maria Tallchief records some of the hardships Balanchine experienced during what he called that "awful, brutal period." The Russian people "suffered more than you can imagine," he told her. When the theaters were permitted to operate again, she goes on, and George returned to the Maryinsky, conditions were intolerable in the formerly well-funded school. There was no food and there was no heat. "We almost froze," he told her. "We could see our breath onstage. At night in school we burned wood parquet floors for fuel and made trousers out of draperies." It was winter in the north of Russia, but extreme hunger won out over the cold: "We were starving. . . . One time it was so bad, students so hungry, we cooked dead cat from street and ate it."[3] Tallchief concludes this account with a recollection of Balanchine's chronic nightmares.

You begin to see the history woven into the ballets, so diverse, made in 1954. Isn't it possible that the "dancers costumed in bandages and as cadavers" of *Opus 34* were in some way linked to that "awful, brutal period" in Balanchine's life? Did such a linkage, in Mr. B's mind, prompt—or necessitate?—that rehearsal of gruesome scenes in the Schoenberg directly before he began choreographing *Nutcracker*? Years earlier, did that same linkage engender the "military slave-drivers lashing forced labor" in the Gluck *Orfeo*? This is pure speculation, but it accords with Balanchine's repeated engagement with the Orpheus myth, the myth of the musician who charms his way into the region of dead souls in order to retrieve his beloved. An ancient mythos dating back to fertility rites and dying gods, the descent of Isis, Inanna, Ishtar, Astarte to the underworld to raise up Osiris, Dumuzi, Adonis, Tammuz, to new life. Maybe the twelve-tone nightmare ballet was Balanchine's "sop to Cerberus," so to speak, a species of entrance fee. Maybe the bandages and corpses and terrifying operations of the Schoenberg were a prerequisite; perhaps they constituted the first stage of a journey to the past, the dead past. Maybe they enabled the Orphic choreographer to retrieve his lush, magical production of *The Nutcracker* from the lost region of the Russian Imperium.

14

Mostly Mo - tz - art

ANNY SAID, laughing, that George had everyone mystified the evening before at charades. "He gave us a three-
syllable word " she explained, firmly closing the door to her locker,
"the name of a composer and *nobody* could get it; we tried everything!" We were in the girls' dressing room at the School getting
ready either for class or rehearsal. "Can you imagine who it *was*?"
she demanded sounding scandalized. No, we couldn't guess who
the three-syllable composer was either, since it wasn't Stravinsky
or Tchaikovsky or Beethoven or Mendelssohn or Hindemith. Ah!
Vivaldi! NO. Bellini? NO. We tried a couple of long shots: Jay - Ess -
Bach? Her - shy Kay? No, no. We gave up. Who then?

Tanny was about twenty-four at the time and had known Mr. B
ever since she was in children's class at the School. Her mother
and father had separated. Edith Le Clercq, an elegant woman with
coiffed silver hair, accompanied her daughter during our first European tours. Jacques Le Clercq was a scholar, a specialist in medieval
French literature and poetry, who was rumored to have lost himself

in drink. In the mid-1950s he had dedicated to Tanaquil a selection (in translation) of the poems of François Villon, the fifteenth-century poet-thief, which I happened upon many years later. His daughter, born in France, had received her education at the Lycée Française in New York; she spoke French as fluently as English, was extremely sensitive to language and had a positive genius for crossword puzzles. Tanny could be exclusive and bitchy and withdrawn. She could be friendly, entertaining, and surprisingly warm, especially with people she was close to. And she was a born actress. She and Balanchine had been married for less than a year at this point, but Tanny answered us in the married woman's long-suffering tone of voice—tolerant, with just a tincture, the merest hint of disdain. The tone reserved for hubby's minor foibles. *Three* syllables, she reiterated, shooting up three fingers one at a time as she articulated each of them separately: "MO - TZ - ART."

Maybe Mr. B was being inventive at the game of charades; maybe it was his not-so-perfect English. Most likely—I wouldn't put it past him—he was simply cheating to gain an advantage. Describing his impressions of Stravinsky and Balanchine in the *New York Review of Books*, Robert Craft (who, in an earlier writing, had brilliantly characterized Balanchine's "plant-like hands") cited his "tendency to omit verbs and the ends of sentences" at about this time. But as I recall, by 1953 to 1954 Mr. B had pretty much arrived at the "resourceful, fluent, original, and not quite correct" use of English that Craft ascribes to the later years.[1] Whether it was his "originality," or the wish to mystify that prompted the three-syllable Mozart, I'd already come to the conclusion that Mr. Balanchine's idea of number was vastly different from ours.

Not long before, between matinee and evening performances, he'd sat down for coffee with a few of us who were grabbing a sandwich or a quick omelette at the little "greasy spoon" directly across from the backstage entrance to the theater. The one on West 56th Street we called "Julie's" although the sign on the window read "Francine's." He'd squeezed into a booth that already held four and joined a session of "What bird or animal is so-and-so?" This one was a donkey. That one a badger, a panther, a camel, a frog, a plump pigeon, a puppy, a peacock, a mole. We giggled, turned one of the principals into an ostrich; another became a weeping-willow tree. This was a collaborative effort until Mr. B characterized my friend Basia (Barbara Walczak) as a porcupine. "What kind of animal is Barbara?" Basia asked Balanchine, meaning me. He peers at me, taking his time, with his head slightly cocked to one side. Then this nasty teasing expression spreads over his face. I'm in for it! "Well, dear" he finally answers, addressing me directly, "you are one-half *monkey*." I don't much care for this. "And one-half *cat*." This I like. I'm about to suggest we move on to somebody else but he's not finished: "And you are one-half *mushroom*, delicious *soft mushroom!*" He smiles wickedly, knows he's got under my skin. I'm so mad I spit back, "And *you*, you're a . . . you're a . . . musical *chipmunk*! And you can't have three halves!" But you can. You certainly can. Especially if you're George Balanchine and tend to think outside the box. Think "Mo-tz-art" in three syllables.

One hundred and fifty years separated Balanchine from Mozart, but both were born in January, only five days apart; both were *Aquarians*—the astrological House of Genius—and both had genial music in their DNA. Each was the brightest star of a musical family. Edwin Denby carried the aesthetic parallel further. In 1945, he writes: "By asking his dancers to do what they best can, by allowing each to be independently interesting, by following the emotional overtones of the rhythm and line of a human body in action," Balanchine "leaves the dancer his naturalness, his freshness, his dignity. The secrets of emotion he reveals are like those of Mozart, tender, joyous, and true."[2]

I'd known from rehearsals of my very first ballet, back in 1946, that Mozart and Balanchine spoke the same language. In *Symphonie Concertante*, the concerto scored for violin, viola, and chamber orchestra, Balanchine had set a *pas de trois* to the slow central movement—Mozart's poignant, throbbing love poem—that somehow rendered visible both the passion *and* the classical purity of the music. In 1952 (the year before the charade party), he'd added *Caracole* to the repertoire—a spirited series of variations to Mozart's Divertimento No. 15 in B-flat major. The dancers wore

festive plumes for headgear and the ballet, with its equine orien-
tation, may well have originated as Balanchine's courtly salutation
to the famous Spanish Riding Academy in Mozart's Austria. Three
years later, in the spring of 1956, we performed a revised version
of *Caracole*—renamed *Divertimento No. 15*—for the Mozart Bicentennial at the Shakespeare Theatre in Stratford, Connecticut,
along with "A Musical Joke" and the "Serenade for Thirteen Wind
Instruments." The well-known Erich Leinsdorf conducted. Leinsdorf, while an excellent choice for Mozart, had a microscopic beat.
If you were dancing at a fast pace, it was hard to follow the delicate
fluctuations of his wrists and fingers. We weren't alone. During orchestra rehearsal, one exasperated musician pulled out a telescope
and squinted into it to make the point. The musicians, who had a
strong union, were always braver than we were.

Mozart's "musical joke" and Balanchine's choreographic reflection of it turned on unexpected, almost painful, dissonances; it required an appreciation of strict polyphonic logic on the one hand,
and a Modernist sense of humor on the other. We didn't bring *Ein
Musikalischer Spass* back to New York but *Divertimento No. 15* re-
joined the repertoire. (As it happens, I replaced Allegra Kent, who
had sadly contracted measles, at the City Center premiere of *Divertimento*. And while I could not help but feel something of an in-
terloper, I did love dancing with Roy Tobias, who was exquisitely
musical and an expert partner, and was tickled by one reviewer
who wrote that in my solo variation I was "as bouncy as a baby on
a rubber mattress.")

This was the year to celebrate Mozart. Five months earlier, in
January of 1956, Balanchine had directed the staging of *The Magic
Flute* for the NBC Opera Theatre. This was the first full-length opera
to be to be produced for American television. Mozart's *Magic Flute*
would be aired in vivid color at a time when TV was largely black
and white. It was a serious undertaking, an "American first," and
Lincoln Kirstein was deeply involved in the project. The libretto was
cast into English from the original German by W. H. Auden and
his partner Chester Kallman. (Auden insisted this was not a "translation" but a *transliteration*. That is, the poet was using English

Premiere of *Divertimento No. 15* at the New York City Center of Music and Drama (November 1957). *Kneeling (left to right):* Barbara Walczak, Diana Adams, Melissa Hayden, Jillana, Barbara Milberg. *Standing (left to right):* Nicholas Magallanes, Jonathan Watts, Roy Tobias. Photograph by Fred Fehl with permission of Gabriel Pinski, www.FredFehl.com. Courtesy New York City Ballet Archive.

words that as much as possible contained the sounds, especially the vowels, sung in German.) The two were close friends with Lincoln and they haunted the rehearsal studios in their British tweed hats. Auden's face was permanently flushed and deeply seamed; it had the look of a snapshot that had been crumpled up and then spread out again. Lincoln, in the role of "Special Production Assistant," was determined to make the production as authentic as possible. He personally engaged the three reedy-voiced little boys who discharged in a "pure" but faintly quavering register the part of the three Guiding Spirits usually sung by female sopranos.

Most of our rehearsals took place at NBC-TV's Brooklyn studios where there was plenty of space, and the opera was telecast on January 15 from that same location. Balanchine had cast me as one of the three Ladies who attend the Queen of the Night in *The Magic Flute*, for the same reason, I expect, that he made me the first Snowflake to appear on stage in *The Nutcracker*. I was "the musical one" who could count out the measures before our entrance. In the NBC production, we three dancers had to learn the entire vocal part sung by the Ladies of the Night. We actually mouthed the words as we performed simple movements, and the cameras were focused on us. In another part of the studio, squashed together in a small sound-proofed chamber, three invisible singers sent their voices into a microphone and that's what the audience heard. It must have been convincing because long after the telecast, I received surprised compliments on my "trained voice." I have to say that, with the exception of well-known singers such as Leontyne Price, who sang *Pamina*, none of us were paid very well, but I came away from that production with an unexpected bonus. After weeks and weeks of rehearsals, of incessant stopping and starting, of standing idly by as each act was staged and all the parts sung again and again, I had absorbed the score and had just about every note of Mozart's *Magic Flute* by heart.

Balanchine had a definite philosophy with respect to the staging of Mozart opera. I'd learned this the year before, sometime in 1955, when he and Tanny graciously accepted my invitation to dinner—*Chinese* dinner—to be cooked in my brand-new wok. They didn't have far to walk from their spacious apartment on West 79th Street and Broadway to my place on 78th near Riverside. The Chinese dishes turned out to be . . . shall we say "edible"? . . . after a series of near disasters, but I had neglected to provide my guests with anything stronger than tea to drink. Luckily, the Balanchines brought a bottle of brandy as a house gift, so we opened it right away and before long a truly Mozartian *Gemütlichkeit* warmed the room. It turned into quite an evening.

I'd invited a couple of friends who lived in my building—a nice old brownstone that no longer exists—to join us, and help with the cooking. Nicole, a tiny attractive person with dark hair, bright eyes, and a voice in the *coloratura* range, was studying opera. She was also a terrific cook. Lenny, her husband, was a huge good-looking insurance salesman. He and Mr. B got very chummy in a corner, and to this day I cannot imagine what they found to discuss so vigorously. Tanny was really nice and offered to help chop the vegetables. She seemed to have intuited that I'd never prepared Chinese food before in my life. We cooked and drank and told stories and, finally, ate. I began to relax.

After dinner, Balanchine was inspired to talk about the way Mozart was usually staged, a happy subject, I thought, considering how little else the group had in common. I had no idea, at this juncture, that he was actually preparing to stage *The Magic Flute*. "Like cartoon, like *Disney*" he informs the rest of us, sniffing scornfully, "Singer must run here, hide there." He pantomimes a character bent nearly double while creeping around a column, attempting to sing his part. I move the dinner table and chairs out of the way. Mr. B disappears behind my draperies, sings several bars of music in a muffled voice, then emerges with a dramatic flourish: "Singers cannot sing! Lose *pep*! Every note, must do something else." He mimes a frantic singer who is forced to gesture or assume a new posture on every note of music. Nicole, the voice student, is glowing; she nods approvingly. Balanchine now pushes the four of us together in the middle of the floor and lines us up side by side, shoulders touching. A quartet; full frontal view. "Now you can hear" he says, in calm tones of reason. We reel back to our seats but Mr. B, carried away, now pantomimes each member of the quartet in turn: soprano, contralto, tenor, bass. Each one stands tall with head up, mouth open, facing front. Clearly, they are singing together, their voices directed straight to the audience. "Now" says the Master, "you can hear Mozart! No runaround, just *wonderful* music." The Balanchine philosophy.

In the summer of that Bicentennial year, the New York City Ballet began a three-month European tour in Mozart's birthplace. We performed at the Festspielhaus during the Salzburg Music Festival from August 26 to 30; after which we were heading to Vienna. We would be the first foreign company to perform at the Staatsoper, Vienna's newly rebuilt opera house, which boasted a "Papageno Room," a beautiful reception hall hung with tapestries depicting scenes from Mozart operas. Back in Salzburg I hadn't got to visit the famous Salt Mines, but I did get to hear Mozart. Mr. B had heard me whistling *Magic Flute* on and off since the NBC production. I had, in fact, become quite proficient at the Queen of the Night's second aria (transposed to a slightly lower key); it was Beethoven quartets I had real trouble whistling. In Salzburg, Mr. Balanchine approached me somewhat diffidently. "Von Karajan is conducting *Magic Flute*," he said, then hesitated for a moment. He knew my parents were Russian Jews. My father, who spoke a beautiful fluent Russian, had visited the School once when we were still Ballet Society, and he and Balanchine had carried on a long conversation in that language. Now he looked at me inquiringly. "It will be good. Do you want to go to matinee with me?" So I walked across the bridge over the rushing Salzburg River with Mr. Balanchine grasping my elbow, and together at the Concert Hall we listened to that Nazi conducting the most angelic music on earth.

15

A Pep Talk

 E'RE IN ANTWERP, doing a rare one-night stand after a couple of days in Brussels. It's the middle of October 1956, and we're due to open at the Paris Opera in two days. Is it returning to Paris that's making Mr. B so uptight? He's nitpicking and moody. Ever since we hit Belgium he's been making trivial changes. Nothing is quite as he wants it to be. Even his favorite dancers cannot satisfy this abrupt perfectionism. Everything is *lousy*. Nobody has any *pep*. What could be driving him to this extreme negativity? If anyone knew, they weren't saying.

This was the trip we called the "German tour," just as 1953 was the year of the "Italian tour." We were at the exact midpoint of a grueling three months of performances and travel with the usual quota of unpredictable injuries, sicknesses, and quick replacements. And although we didn't know it, there was worse yet to come. You could speculate that our choreographer's grumpiness wasn't about Paris at all. Maybe there were personal problems? A rumor had surfaced that Mr. B and Tanny were on the verge of breaking up. What I couldn't know, at this point, was that Balanchine was grappling with a terrible fear. I didn't know that his beloved Stravinsky was in a hospital in Berlin, that he'd suffered a severe stroke just two weeks earlier, and Balanchine had been told that he might not live. With the exception of the immediate staff and the people closest to him, most of us had no idea of the anxiety that was preying on Balanchine's mind.

At this point, the Company had already danced in Austria and Switzerland, then returned to Venice in September for a week of performances. Seated outside at the Taverna la Fenice adjacent to the theater, we indulged in enormous grilled *funghi*, seasonal fall mushrooms the size of a dinner plate, and *pesce al' fiamme*, large fresh peach-halves, pitted and stuffed with nuts and raisins and served *flambée*. After Venice, luminous, rat-ridden, slowly sinking Venice, came Germany: first Berlin, then Munich, Frankfurt, and Cologne. I had done a bad thing in Berlin.

Berlin in 1956 was a conquered city "occupied" by Allied military forces, and divided into American, British, French, and Soviet sectors. It was a city further divided by a severe conflict of ideologies. This was the period of the Cold War, barely ten years after the end of World War II. The major antagonists were the two superpowers capable of building an arsenal of nuclear weapons: the United States and the Union of Soviet Socialist Republics. In less than five years, the Berlin Wall—a concrete barrier nearly twelve feet high and barricaded with barbed wire—would surround West Berlin, physically separating the Soviet East Sector under Russian command from the far more prosperous West Sector. But an invisible wall had already gone up by the time we came to perform in Berlin. From our very first visit, in 1952, it had been made very clear that we were not to leave the Western Sector on our own. During the fifties, before embarking on each of our post-war European tours, all members of the New York City Ballet were instructed to attend USIS (United States Information Service) sessions where we learned that we were to consider ourselves "diplomats." We were expected to attend various functions; told not to sound off on our own, to avoid expressing personal political opinions; and to behave in a way that would uphold the honor of our country. In the occupied zones, we were not to attempt expeditions outside our designated sector.

I had done a bad thing in Berlin. Acting on an erroneous tip, I had taken a strictly *verboten* subway ride to the East Sector in search of Nefertiti. I'd been told there were periodic but infrequent checks of subway riders, so I retrieved my passport from the hotel desk and carried it with me. After plowing fruitlessly through acres of deserted museum buildings, observing whole villas that had been lifted out of Pompeii, corridors lined on both sides with Assyrian lions striding head to tail, I queried a uniformed guard who had been shadowing me at a distance. He informed me rather gruffly that the famous Egyptian head was *nicht hier*, no longer in the collection. It had been moved, he indicated, gesturing toward the West Sector. Back to the *U-Bahn*. I hurried out of the Archaeological Museum, passed endless lines of drab-looking, ill-dressed people waiting for a ration of sausage, got suspicious sidelong glances, and grabbed the first train back to the West Sector where we were quartered.

I had forgotten that this was a dangerous city, that the last time we danced in Berlin my passport was stolen right out of my suitcase on closing night (from a first-class hotel on *Kurfurstendam*, no less), and that Mr. B had held up our plane's departure for home the following morning while a new one was issued to me at the American Consulate.

Betty Cage and Barbara Horgan—Betty's treasured assistant— were not overjoyed at my irresponsible spree. "Horgie" had twice gone under the Wall herself, she told me many years later, once safely with Ruth Sobotka who spoke impeccable German (Ruthie had grown up in Vienna, but fled to America with her parents when the Nazis came to power). The second time, the intrepid Horgan had gone into the Russian Sector alone, as I had done, and found the train diverted and stopped on the return trip. A man standing very close to her had whispered "*Get off* the train. Now!" Asking no questions, she shot out of the station and took a cab back to the office. By the time I waltzed back from the East Sector, she well understood just how dangerous it could be.

Roy Tobias, one of those souls blessed with near-perfect recall, also let me know (nearly half a century later, via email from Seoul) that he too had gone with Sobotka to the East Sector. They were accompanied by Edwina Seaver, known affectionately as "Ducky," one of the most glamorous members of the troupe. "Edwina came with us," he wrote. "Ruth said to dress inconspicuously. Edwina chose heeled pumps, a Humphrey Bogart trench coat, cinched to a 19-inch waist. With the collar turned up, she was about as inconspicuous as Greta Garbo in Central Park. What is more," he added, "she adored everything, the little cubicles with the single hanging light bulb, and the day care center where you left the children while you worked in the factory."

And I thought I was the only one with *hutspah*. At the time, both Horgan and Betty were handling problems far more serious then my little escapade. They knew that Stravinsky had been raced to the hospital and was not expected to survive. They were trying to sustain Mr. B, to keep up his spirits, while taking care of all the other business they had on hand. Betty took the time, however, to soundly reprimand me. We were *not* in Europe to spark international incidents. I'd attended the USIS briefings, hadn't I? I was not there to make trouble. Every dancer in the company was considered an ambassador of sorts. And this was *Berlin*. What was I thinking! What if I'd got caught? Detained? Who would replace me if . . . ?

They were right. I'd been thoughtless; willful, impulsive, and obstinate. More than usual. Genuinely remorseful (especially as I hadn't been able to see Nefertiti), I determined to forego the thrills of disobedience and behave. I behaved beautifully in Brussels, where several of us went to hear Rosalyn Tureck play an all-Bach concert between performances. But like everyone else, I couldn't help noticing how Mr. Balanchine was growing grumpier and more moody with every passing day. It really wasn't like him. You expected Jerry to dump on the dancers, but not Mr. B. In Antwerp I was struck with a brilliant idea! I would make up for the Berlin escapade. I would do something good for the company. It would make a big difference in Paris and everyone would be grateful.

After our class at the Royal Flemish Opera House, which nobody could pronounce in Flemish, I walked straight up to Balanchine and asked if we might go for coffee somewhere close by, just the two of us. I said I wanted very much to speak with him in private—it wouldn't take very long. I was emboldened, partly because he'd almost always taken the trouble to answer my questions, and partly because I'd recently been designated a soloist. The year before, in 1955, Carolyn George, Barbara Walczak, Barbara Fallis, and I had received formal billing; our names were printed just under the principals' names in all the program booklets and flyers.

It had been a gradual and arduous rise for me. It began in 1951, when Mr. B assigned me the role of Leto who, in the opening scene of *Apollo*, gives birth to the god on top of a precarious, shaky mountain. I think Balanchine picked me for the part because it was common knowledge that I had terrible cramps every month. He probably figured I'd already had plenty of experience with labor pains and I have to admit I *was* pretty good as Apollo's mom—especially after Nan Porcher, the stage manager, installed a handle for me to grip while I was flinging around. I must have been more graphic in the part than the dancers before me with their polite writhings, because after the first few performances—I still relish the moment!—Balanchine sidled up to me one evening and joked that I was the best mother he ever had!

A year later, having done my apprenticeship as a corps de ballet Monster, and then a Maiden in *Firebird*, I was given the role of the Russian Princess-Bride. I was not quite as tall and imposing as my predecessors, but according to Mr. Balanchine I looked the part. Like "pretty little Georgian girl," he told me. In the grand wedding scene that closes the ballet, he taught us to bow straight down from the waist without bending our knees, left arm motionless at the side, right hand placed over the left shoulder, then swept down with open palm until the fingertips touch the floor. (It wasn't until I attended a memorial service for Balanchine at the Russian Church on East 97th Street, years later, that I saw the officiating priest bend repeatedly in that very same bow and realized it was a ritual obeisance.) By 1953, I was doing demi-solos in *Four Tempera-*

ments and the first movement of *Symphony in C*. In Bizet, the two demi-soloists are expected to dance in unison. Vida Brown came up to our dressing room one night to give us notes and corrections. "You are jumping too high," she cautioned me earnestly, "and doing three *pirouettes* instead of two—and you're holding the balance too long." Ruth Sobotka turned to Vida poker-faced, and sweetly queried, "Why don't you make her a soloist?" I choked.

The following year I got a real break. Melissa Hayden had taken a temporary leave of absence, and I inherited the sexy role of "Profane Love" in Freddy Ashton's *Illuminations*, a ballet celebrating the poet Rimbaud. I don't think anyone could match the precision and intensity that Melissa brought to the role, and I had nowhere near her seemingly effortless technique, but for me it was a rare principal part; it brought good notices. "Barbara Milberg has really come to grips with the role of Profane Love" wrote the *Times'* reviewer: "She has found not only its essential sensuality, but also its inner violence, and she plays it in exciting style."[1] That same year Balanchine paired me with Roy Tobias, and we whirled around the stage together in the opening section of Ravel's mysterious, swooning "Valses Nobles et Sentimentales" in *La Valse*.

By 1956, I had not only become "strong, violent, and voluptuous" as the figure of Profane Love but was again soaring around the stage, this time in Balanchine's version of *Swan Lake*, in the Pas de Trois originally choreographed for the buoyant Patricia Wilde and two attendant swans. Both in New York and during our "German tour," I was replacing Carolyn George d'Amboise who, at this point, was waiting out the term of the d'Amboises' first baby. The Pas de Trois was not only a principal role but a show-stopper —and nearly a heart-stopper: I invariably ended up gasping for breath in the wings after the final series of split-jumps. (Balanchine cut the part out of *Swan Lake* the season after I left the company.) But I will always remember how Jerry Robbins came up personally, after my first performance of it in New York, to praise me with real admiration in his voice. "You really floated!" he said. I was astonished. With the exception of *The Guests*, the first ballet he did for NYCB in 1949, and later *Fanfare*, Jerry had repeatedly

Barbara Milberg as "Profane Love" in Frederick Ashton's *Illuminations* (1954). Photograph by Maurice Seymour, courtesy Ron Seymour.

Milberg as "Profane Love" in *Illuminations*. Photograph by Maurice Seymour, courtesy Ron Seymour.

cast me in almost all of his ballets and then repeatedly cast me out of them, sometimes more than once, for reasons unfathomable to anyone but himself.

I'd worked hard for solo billing, but I also felt that Balanchine had been generous. I didn't have the long shapely legs and feet with high insteps that he prized, but I did have a nice long neck, could jump and turn, move with speed and grace—and I understood "grand manner." Mr. B knew I was musical and good at dramatic parts; he'd given me roles I could develop and dance well. But there was another reason that made me think, in Antwerp, that Mr. B would hear me out.

A few years back I'd fallen in love with a Pergolesi *Concertina*. I wanted to set a dance to the delicate Baroque music and Balanchine told me to go ahead, ask some people to work with me. He would give me the small studio at the School to work in, and see if Simon Sadoff was willing to play for us. "If you want to move people" he said, looking at me searchingly, "well then, you must." Then he said something that surprised me. He told me to remember, always, that a dancer's beautiful arabesque was not my choreography, that she had worked on it for years and that I could not take credit for it. I got eight dancers to work with me and Simon to play, and choreographed the first movement. Mr. B came to see the results and that practice bout led to a grander scheme.

I would choreograph *Dracula*; that thrilling vampire story I'd read in London at the Voronine's dreary establishment. Nobody had done a real horror ballet since *Giselle*. I'd set it to Bartok's *Music for Percussion, Celeste, and Strings*, very spooky. Mr. B thought not. So I changed over to the Bartok *Concerto for Two Pianos and Percussion*. Spooky and dramatic. No place to put two pianos, said Mr. B. I was considering Bartok's fifth string quartet when somebody had the kindness to tell me that Balanchine disliked Bartok. However, Lincoln was interested in a young Hawaiian composer, D. K. Lee, who had written a score using "Waltzing Mathilda" as its thematic base. He and Mr. B persuaded me to "at least try it."

That year, I was not the only one experimenting with choreography. One paper reported, under the heading "Five Dancers Creating New Ballets" that "Jacques d'Amboise, Barbara Milberg, Shaun O'Brian, Herbert Bliss and Francisco Moncion are preparing their ballets to music which ranges from Rieti's Fifth symphony through a contemporary Hawaiian score to Mozart." Kirstein and Balanchine encouraged the ventures by arranging for us to have accompanists and rehearsal space—often the City Center stage itself. Unhappily for me, and the dancers who'd given time and energy to the project, Count Dracula and Waltzing Mathilda refused to be joined in unholy matrimony. The horror ballet was scrapped. But shortly after, in 1955, Balanchine suggested that Moncion and I each set one of the dances in *Jeux d'Enfants*, a new ballet. I chose the fable of "The Lion and the Mouse" to choreograph, and persuaded Eugene Tanner and "Evil Annie" (Ann Crowell Inglis), respectively, to dance the lion and mouse roles. (Annie was christened "Evil" because she swore like the proverbial trouper. The

Sketch of Lion costume (including mouse) by designer Esteban Frances for *Jeux d'Enfants* (1955), choreography by George Balanchine, Francisco Moncion, and Barbara Milberg. From author's collection.

girls in the big dressing room framed her mirror with holy pictures, but it didn't elevate her vocabulary.) Gene was leonine to start with, and a good partner; Esteban Frances designed a bewhiskered golden lion suit for him. Lithe blue-eyed Annie learned steps almost faster than I could invent them, and *Jeux d'Enfants* stayed in the repertoire for quite a while, with "choreography by George Balanchine, Francisco Moncion, and Barbara Milberg."

So that was why I had the nerve to approach Mr. B with my grand plan, my inspiration, after our class in Antwerp. Yes, he said, rather surprised, he could take a little time to speak with me. Within the hour, I found myself at a nearby café seated across from my somewhat-less-grumpy choreographer at an outdoor table. Now he seemed inquisitive. What was on my mind? Would I like something to drink? Coffee?

I heard myself telling him the simple truth. That we were *all* anxious to make a good impression in Paris. That I'd noticed how negative he was lately. I said he was making everybody nervous. His attitude was really depressing; it was making us dance worse, not better. We were fatigued, really tired, I pointed out, and doing our best. Maybe, I offered hopefully, he could do what baseball and football coaches do with their teams before a game? "Mr. B" I pleaded, "you're driving us all nuts! It's not good for morale. What we need is a *pep talk.*"

He looks blank. "A pep talk."

"Yeah," says I, allowing a little Flatbush to creep into my delivery. After all, hadn't I grown up in the land of the Brooklyn Dodgers? Ebbets Field? "Like American sports coaches give their teams right before a game. It makes them want to go out there and *win*. It gives them *pep!*" I hoped "American" would turn the trick.

"I never do this. I don't know what is pep talk. . . ."

He was actually listening. It's easy, I said. Just get everybody together before the performance tonight and tell us how *good* we are. "Be like a football coach," I advised. "Say we are the *best* company, and that we are going to *wow* them in Paris. Say they will *love* us. That you believe in us. *You can do that.*" I told him earnestly, applying a little "pep psychology" of my own. "It will make a *big* difference. You'll see."

That evening, an announcement came over the public address system: Mr. Balanchine wants everybody, the whole company, to come on stage fifteen minutes before curtain time. When we had assembled, he delivered his pep talk. It was a bomb. He meandered around for a while telling us he knew we were tired, but that was what you should expect if you want to be in professional company. Anyway, we would be okay in Paris. We would be fine, and we weren't going to be there very long so don't worry about it. Nobody expected us to be better than we were, he said. We should just work hard but be careful, try not to have accident and be replaced. We were all "nice people." It went something like that.

The collected dancers of the New York City Ballet stood listening to this with expressionless faces. A few looked puzzled. Had they been called on stage early just to hear this morose, somewhat rambling talk? They drifted back to dressing rooms in twos and threes. A few hooked on to the most solid thing in sight and began to warm up. I felt profoundly grateful. Mr. Balanchine had delivered his "pep talk" without mentioning whose brilliant idea it was.

16

Nightmare in Copenhagen

ETTY CAGE, our business manager, was a striking woman. She had black hair, wide-set bottomless black eyes, a broad face with good bones, and a complexion that ranged from pale to tan. She appeared to have an admixture of Native American and African bloodlines along with the Caucasian, but could easily have passed as a gypsy. Surrounded by skinny people, Betty tended more toward plumpness; she wore comfortable black clothing and bore an uncanny resemblance to a large black pussycat—with the feline's built-in smile. And while she could be devious, also like the cat, it was hard not to like her.

With Barbara Horgan, and the help of Eddie Bigelow, Betty ran the office on the eighth floor of the City Center Building with placid assurance, calmly smoothing irritations and unknotting the problems that constantly arose. Bigelow was Balanchine's right-hand man and liaison with the staff. He was a laconic Yankee from Massachusetts who took care of just about anything that required doing. Eddie was the carpenter who crated Mr. B's Vespa in Florence; the dancer who appeared on stage as Von Rothbart, the Sorcerer in *Swan Lake*, the Mouse King in *Nutcracker*, and as Pluto, god of the Underworld, in *Orpheus*; Bigelow was the friend who took me home to Brooklyn in a cab when I severely sprained an ankle in class. And I will never forget that afternoon at the City Center when Eddie marched into dressing room #7—empty except for me—with the *Peloponnesian War* in his hand, parked himself at the next dressing table, and with a kind of grim relish read out Thucydides' celebrated description of the plague that devastated Athens. He was devoted to Mr. B and worked with Betty and Horgie in the office when needed.

Fortunately, Betty possessed a sense of humor as well as competence; she handled a myriad trivial and not-so-trivial concerns that would have driven lesser souls hysterical. I can still hear those amused, ironic tones repeating *"No good deed goes unpunished!"*—her mantra. In temperament, Betty was a combination of the sanguine and phlegmatic "humours." Each week, at home and on tour, she cheerfully handed us our paychecks; and so far as I know, she never lost patience with any of us. Whether it was a nervous Lincoln, a beset Mr. B, or a bewildered new member of the corps, she directed her attention to each individual with the same pragmatic serenity. Betty, we thought, was a witch—a good witch. *And* she was psychic.

Several times I'd attended informal séances at her walk-up on Third Avenue along with Eddie and Horgie and a few friends. Bigelow was more inclined to relax with a drink and talk to people than to investigate the paranormal. Horgie also enjoyed Betty's gatherings but didn't go in much for the séance stuff either, thought the whole thing "too intense." The rest of us sipped red wine, nibbled on hors d'oeuvres, consulted the Ouija board, and heard indistinct table-knockings. In between, we passed around tales of ghastly appearances, sudden drops in temperature, ghostly hand-prints in hot wax, and various other occult manifestations. Every so often a train on the "El" would rumble by. We gathered around the table with our palms down, fingers spread out, our hands touching in an unbroken circuit; in the flickering light of candles we asked questions of the Spirits. I remember gasps, one evening, when the table canted to one side at a sudden terrifying angle.

Betty's real gift was for reading the Tarot cards, although she didn't care to do it too often. She was very good at interpreting the configurations of the Higher Arcana—allegorical images of *Death, the Lovers, the Falling Tower, the Wheel of Fortune, the Hermit, the Jester,* and so forth—and analyzing the disposition of the numbered cards in the deck, Cups and Staves, Swords and Pentacles. Once she laid out the Tarot deck in a short version for me when I pressed her *please* to "tell my fortune." When she'd finished turning over the cards, we saw that the vertical axis at the center had the *Popess* at the apex of the column and the *Devil* at the base. I was mystified, but Betty said I had the choice to go either way—or could go both ways. A prescient reading.

Over a period of years Betty had grown more and more adept, not only in readings of character but in predicting changes, dangers, and the probable outcome of some tangled turn of events. Some people have twenty-twenty eyesight; Betty had twenty-twenty insight. That's why we called her "psychic." And that was why (as I heard soon after from people close to her, and learned from Betty herself many years later) she deliberately equivocated when, in Berlin, during the 1956 "German Tour," Tanaquil persuaded her to lay out the Tarot cards and read her fortune. The forecast was ominous. And painful for Betty. She could not tell Tanny she had seen catastrophe. She was desperately hoping she was wrong.

We'd been traveling north and toward winter at the same time. After closing in Berlin on the first of October, our itinerary took us to Munich, Frankfurt, Brussels, Antwerp, Paris, Cologne, and finally Scandinavia. We were scheduled to perform in Copenhagen during the last week of October, then go on to Stockholm for a week ending in mid-November. The days had grown shorter as we traveled. Every day the dark closed in a little sooner than the day before, and every day it grew colder.

We arrived in Copenhagen by train, settled into our hotels, received invitations to a royal party in our honor, and opened as planned on the twenty-sixth of October at the Kongelige Teater.

There were the usual Company classes, and a couple of brief rehearsals to accommodate to the stage. The tour was nearly over. Some of us traveled to Elsinore, some miles north of Copenhagen, to visit the castle of Kronborg (the original of Shakespeare's "Elsinore") and I was disappointed to find that Hamlet's castle was not what I'd imagined—that is, a ghost-ridden Gothic stronghold perched on craggy cliffs at the edge of a wind-tormented North Sea—but a spare symmetrical structure of hewn rock housing a maritime museum. In Copenhagen, the famous Tivoli Gardens were closed for the winter, but we did find Hans Christian Andersen's Little Mermaid perched on a rock in the bay, her tail intact.

At the theater, after the first few days, there was a growing sense that something was wrong. Mr. Balanchine was missing a good deal of the time. Todd was teaching Company class. Eddie Bigelow went about his business and danced his usual parts but grew gloomier and more laconic as the days and hours passed. A general malaise began to spread through the Company. I don't remember exactly which night it was—was it opening night?—that an anxious Yvonne Mounsey stood in for Tanaquil in *Divertimento*. She was hastily replaced in *Swan Lake*. *Bourrée Fantasque*. Another ballet was substituted for *La Valse*. Tanny couldn't dance. Nobody could tell us exactly what was wrong with her but she was ill, very ill. Muscle cramps. Weakness. Headache. Fever.

News of her condition leaked out sporadically. Annie Inglis learned that Tanny had called out "George! I need to go to the bathroom and I can't get out of bed." Early on, I remember stopping a worried Mr. B who was moving quickly toward the back of the stage, just before the performance, to ask about Tanny and to let him know I had the phone number of a young doctor at the American Hospital. He'd been in the seat next to mine on the train to Copenhagen and given me the hospital number "just in case." Mr. B broke in, told me that a highly recommended massage therapist had been contacted. He was giving Tanny special massage treatments at their hotel. Her mother was with Tanny night and day. He raced off.

The next day the news was terrifying. Tanny was experiencing

excruciating pains in the spine, the fever had mounted to an unbelievable 106 degrees, and a medical doctor had been called in. He
thought she might have contracted spinal meningitis, a sure killer
at the time, and immediately had Tanny removed to the hospital.
Then there was silence. We waited. No more news leaked out. At
least not to the company in general.

But when the diagnosis was final, some people had to be no-
tified immediately. Vida Brown, our Ballet Mistress, was probably the first person—after her husband and her mother—to learn
what disease Tanny had contracted. When Vida told me about it
more than forty years later, I could sense the distress that was
loaded into the remembrance. In Copenhagen, Vida said, she and
Melissa Hayden were sharing a room in the same hotel as the Balanchine party. Every night after the performance they'd gone to
Mr. B to ask how Tanny was doing. Toward the end of that week
they were both fast asleep when Vida heard knocking and got up
to open the door.

As she recalls it, an insistent knocking awakened Vida at 5:30 in
the morning. When she opened the door Mr. B was there, standing
in the hall. He looked drawn, pale, somehow shrunken. Come in,
come in! No, he just stood there speechless in the doorway. "What
is it? What's the matter?" Vida prompted with some urgency. And
Balanchine finally was able to say the words: "It's Tanny. She has
polio." I put my arms around him, said Vida, and he started to cry,
we both started to cry. Then Millie flung her arms around them
both, and all three were weeping. Vida asked if she could order
some coffee, couldn't think what else to do, but the stricken Balanchine didn't respond. He retreated back into the hallway and
leaned against the wall.

We left Denmark, bundled up against the cold, boarding the
ferry from Copenhagen to Malmö in the south of Sweden, then the
train to Stockholm in the north. Somebody, maybe Horgie, photographed me on the ferry; I had on earmuffs and was clutching
a little Steiff leopard I'd acquired on the way. It was strange to be
traveling without Tanny and Mr. B. At some point, either on the
ferry or the train, each of us were handed a letter on U.S. Army let-

terhead, a bald notification that we could be vaccinated against poliomyelitis—if we wanted it—when we arrived in Hamburg, our
take-off point for the United States and home.

Poliomyelitis was the highly contagious disease we knew as "in-
fantile paralysis," the disease that had crippled President Roosevelt. With the exception of Barbara Walczak, who had contracted
and recovered from polio as a child, everyone was pretty scared.
Was the disease already incubating in some of us? How long before we'd know? Several decided to refuse the vaccination offer.
Some of the younger members had already been vaccinated. It
turned out the medics didn't have enough vaccine, in any case,
to innoculate everyone in the company. But at least we knew now
what had happened to Tanny. In Stockholm we learned that she
was still alive. Barely.

She'd been admitted to the American Hospital in Copenhagen
but the prognosis was uncertain; she might or might not recover.
Her mother and Mr. Balanchine were staying with her. She was in
an iron lung. A paralyzed dancer locked up in her own body. How
many years would go by before fifty or sixty dancers would stop
having nightmares?

In the United States polio had been rampant for years. Its first
symptoms could be mistaken for flu, but then the virus attacked
the central nervous system. It wasted muscles, caused paralysis,
crippling, and often death. Children were particularly vulnerable.
The organism that caused the disease had been isolated in 1913,
but it was not until July 1952 that Jonas Salk perfected the vaccine
that bears his name. By 1954 there was mass inoculation of school-
children. In that one year, according to government statistics, the
disease had killed over 1,300 people in the United States alone,
and crippled more than 18,000. In 1955, with rigorous standards
in place, vaccination had reduced the known cases of polio in the
States to approximately 29,000. By 1956, the number had de-
creased by more than half, and 1957 saw fewer than 6,000 cases.
Looking back, it seems a devastating irony that the Salk vaccine
was not one of the multiple inoculations we were *required* to have
before we could leave the country and be allowed to return.

Tanaquil survived, although it was touch and go for a while. Two months after she was stricken, the School sent Natasha Molo (Natalie Molostwoff), one of the administrators and a dear friend of Tanny's, to Copenhagen as a Christmas present. "Tanny was just out of the iron lung," she told Francis Mason, "but she was in despair, in tears. She was white and slack as a piece of paper and scared to death."[1] Mason, well-known dance critic, scholar, editor, ballet historian—and co-author with Mr. B of *Balanchine's Complete Stories of the Great Ballets* and *101 Stories of the Great Ballets*—was collecting interviews from dancers and associates intimate with Balanchine over his life-span, an invaluable collection that remains a prime source of information on the man, certainly the most varied. It was Natasha who revealed, at that time, what most of their intimate friends had long known. Tanny and Balanchine had been on the verge of breaking up and would have separated, she said, if Tanny had not become ill.

They brought her home and Mr. B took her to Warm Springs, Georgia, where Roosevelt had received regular therapy. Tanny was determined to recover as much as possible, and with hard work she gradually regained the use of one arm fully and the other in part. Balanchine continued to work with her, exercise her, but the legs did not recover. She would need a wheelchair to get about. But as we discovered over a period of years, her spirit was anything but crippled.

The woman was indomitable. Collaborating with Martha Swope, the dancer who became one of the great photographers of dance, she wrote a charming whimsical text for *Mourka: The Autobiography of a Cat* (1964), about the house pet Balanchine had trained himself. It was marvelously illustrated by Swope's photographs: Mourka, outdoing the dancers in class. Mourka, spread-eagled in a leap, jumping over Balanchine's crouching form. Mourka, lovingly held in his trainer's arms. A remarkable collaboration among four uniquely gifted individuals.

Jerry Robbins brought her to the theater, carried her when necessary. Eddie Bigelow and Diana Adams were constantly with her. Her friends stayed her friends and she made new ones. For a while,

Cover photo of *Mourka: The Autobiography of a Cat* by Tanaquil Le Clercq Balanchine and Martha Swope (New York: Stein and Day, 1964). Photograph © Martha Swope.

To Barbara — the most beautiful feline-fancier, with all best wishes from.

Mourka + Tanny

Tanny's inscription on the copyright page of *Mourka*. Author's collection.

she taught classes from her wheelchair at Arthur Mitchell's ballet school in Harlem. She was the composer of several crossword puzzles published in the *New York Times*; at least one appeared in the magazine section of the Sunday *Times*. She developed into a fine photographer herself. She entertained. She read. She summered in Connecticut. In January of 1984, with willing helpers, she hosted the fiftieth anniversary of the founding of the School of American Ballet at her West 79th Street apartment.

Out of the blue she sent me a funny little book one Christmas, *Horoscopes for Pussycats*, inscribed on the last page in her own strong hand: "To Barbara—Merry Christmas, all my love—Tanny." How had she remembered—and combined!—my delight in pussycats and early fascination with the occult? A few months after my daughter was born, in 1961, Diana called to ask if I would like to bring the baby over to 79th Street so that Tanny could see her. I had not seen Tanny since before Copenhagen and didn't realize her hair had turned the color of her mother's. She held the infant Alexandra on her lap for a minute but Diana had to help support the weight. Maybe twelve pounds. When *Mourka* came out in 1964, she sent me a copy, this time inscribed on the copyright page to "the most beautiful feline-fancier," from "Mourka + Tanny." She had drawn whiskers, eyes and a mouth on the outsized "M" of "Mourka," and used the peaks of the M to provide ready-made ears.

The last time I saw Tanny was at the Fiftieth Anniversary of the New York City Ballet in 1998. The celebration took place in the State Theater at Lincoln Center and the performance was specially dedicated to Tanaquil Le Clercq. I sat in the balcony with my "generation" of NYCB dancers, and watched as that remarkable woman was greeted by a resounding ovation the moment she appeared in the aisle at the left of the orchestra. We joined the cheering audience as she waved, from her wheelchair, with royal aplomb.

17

A Class of One's Own

ARTHUR MITCHELL joined the company toward the end of 1955. He'd been awarded a scholarship at the School of American Ballet, and also attended the High School of Performing Arts where he'd taken tap dancing along with the usual academic courses. In 1954, he worked for the first time with Balanchine when the choreographer was setting dances for the Broadway musical, *House of Flowers*; and during the fall of 1955, the twenty-one-year-old dancer received a telegram from Lincoln Kirstein inviting him to join NYCB.[1] Lincoln was impressed with Arthur, wanted to see him paired with Tanaquil Le Clercq in the fourth movement of *Western Symphony*. Apparently, Mr. B thought Arthur should first serve an apprenticeship, just as Allegra Kent had, and gain experience in the corps before grappling with a principal role. The fact that Arthur was black doesn't seem to have entered the dialogue. On the other hand, a snatch of conversation between Lincoln and Balanchine, overheard in the Company's administrative offices, may have had everything to do with Arthur's complexion:

LINCOLN (concerned): But what *will* you put him in?
BALANCHINE (two sniffs): *Swan Lake.*

From the outset it was evident that Arthur had "class." That is, he possessed a certain *noblesse*, a noble bearing, at that time a rare quality in young American males. But his skin color fell somewhere between milk-chocolate and coffee and classical ballet companies did not hire black dancers, no matter how good they might be. It was a knotty problem. Balanchine, however, knew the story about Alexander the Great and his solution for untying the Gordian Knot. You don't waste time trying to untie it; you slash it in two. You put Arthur in a "white ballet." *Swan Lake.* No explanations. No fuss. Like Alexander you move on.

So Arthur came into the company as one more member of the corps de ballet. Balanchine did indeed put him in *Swan Lake*—as one of the Hunters, not Prince Siegfried; he was one of two Trumpets in Jerry Robbins's *Fanfare*, a ballet in which dancers represent various instruments in Benjamin Britten's *Young Person's Guide to the Orchestra.* Todd Bolender cast him as an elevator operator in *Souvenirs*, his new ballet set in the lobby of the Plaza Hotel. We didn't see Arthur doing big solo roles. During the 1955/1956 seasons, he learned where things were and which nearsighted dancers to watch out for on stage. Somebody was always losing a contact lens, and I vaguely remember Arthur joining the rest of us who were scouring the stage floor in hopes of retrieving the precious bit of glass. But perhaps most important during this period of apprenticeship, the new dancer was gaining priceless experience in the delicate, hands-on art of partnering.

When Arthur arrived at the School to take his first company class, SAB was still at Madison and 59th Street (it would shortly relocate to the West Side in January 1956). As I recall, our class was in that same large well-lit studio where Mr. B had presented each little Fury, one at a time, to Igor Stravinsky during the first rehearsals for *Orpheus.* The same studio with the same Mason & Hamlin piano that I used to practice on. Kolya was not at the piano this day. I think John Colman, a young pianist and composer, was playing for class.

The company class taught by Balanchine was a very specialized hour and a half, its focus on style and the dynamics of classical technique. That is, how do you make a *grand battement*, or the lowly *tendu* "interesting"? Not by changing the movement itself but by altering its energy quotient. Snap the foot out from fifth position in a *tendu*, point it as hard as you can till you nearly burst a blood vessel, snap it back at the last nanosecond. Dynamics. Or as Mr. B put it: "Not boring." You don't *sink* down in *grand plié* like a collapsing building; you *force* your way to the bottom. Dynamics also involve rhythm. In a high kick, or *grand battement*, the upward swing is easy. You kick as high as you can, without bending the standing leg or throwing your hip out of alignment. It's the comedown that takes energy, and muscle. That up-flung leg must be lowered light as a feather till it softly floats back to fifth position. Just try it at a fast tempo!

With the exception of Virginia Rich, most of us hadn't seen Arthur in class before and we were curious as to what the new kid on the block would be like. ("Ginger," a soft-spoken girl from Atlanta, Georgia, knew Arthur from when they were students together at SAB.) On this day, Arthur walked into the studio wearing black tights, black ballet slippers, white socks and a close-fitting white T-shirt, very trim. Slender, nice shape. Looking neither to the right nor left he walked straight across the room and took his place at the barre. When Mr. B arrived we lined up and stood waiting in a tight first position, one arm lightly holding the barre, feet and knees and hips turned out, back straight, shoulders down, heads up, butt tucked in. Then came the voiced "one . . . two," signaling the free arm to lift up chest high and open to the side, hands slightly curved. Two long-drawn-out chords accompanied the arm movements. Then the deep *pliés* began.

I need to fill in a bit of background here, bring into focus the disturbed cultural surround of the mid-fifties. In the spring of 1954, roughly six months before Arthur appeared in *House of Flowers*, the United States Supreme Court handed down a decision on a case that changed history. In *Brown v. The Board of Education of Topeka*, the highest court in the land had established "the fundamental principle that racial discrimination in public education is unconstitutional," and stirred up a hornets' nest in the South. The eleven states of the old Confederacy published a manifesto against the "unwarranted" decision and engaged in massive delaying tactics. They were encouraged by a President who neglected to add his very considerable weight to the Court's ruling.

The proponents of desegregation were equally determined to enforce the decision and make the necessary changes. In 1954, a twenty-five-year-old Martin Luther King, Jr., was appointed pastor of a Baptist Church in Montgomery, Alabama, a church whose minister and congregation had protested segregation and considered bus boycotting since the early fifties. On December 1, 1955 (possibly the very day Arthur Mitchell walked into his first company class in New York) the now-famous Rosa Parks refused to yield up her seat on a Montgomery bus when ordered by the driver; she was arrested and jailed. Immediately following Parks's one-woman rebellion, King, a powerful orator, sparked a citywide boycott of a bus system that, throughout the South, forced blacks to render up seats to whites on demand. That Montgomery boycott lasted over a year and served as forerunner to the anti-segregation marches in Birmingham, the lunch counter sit-ins and freedom-rides of the early sixties. By 1956, however, bloody encounters and humiliating episodes had occurred all over the South; the Kings' home was bombed. Over a period of two years the conflict had escalated into appalling violence. Black churches were set aflame; there were beatings, there were murders.

The battle was joined at Little Rock, Arkansas. Between May 1954 and March 1956 there had been an endless series of delays, court suits on the part of the Little Rock School Board followed by countersuits by the NAACP. The conflict seemed interminable; it was stroke and counter-stroke, court order and appeal. The rage on both sides boiled over in September 1957 (just three months before the December 1957 opening of *Agon*) when the Supreme Court ordered the admission of nine black students to Little Rock Central High School for the fall term. The Governor of Arkansas had National Guardsmen with guns posted at the entrance to the school. "Blood will run in the streets" he threatened, and the nine students were turned away. Armed Federal troops were dispatched to protect the black students who were now barred from entering by an angry mob—a *thousand* people. In the end, it took one thousand paratroopers and ten thousand National Guardsmen, ordered in by the President, to get nine kids into school.

In the north, even before the 1957 dénoument, the name of the town had become a symbol of violent hatred and racial bigotry. Sometime between 1955 and 1956, "Little Rock," like "Marathon" or "Hiroshima," had become a place-name that meant more than the place. This, then, was the climate in the nation when Arthur arrived at the School of American Ballet to take his first company class.

During the barre exercises, Mr. Balanchine had been moving slowly around the room stopping here and there to correct a position, lift a drooping elbow. Very soon we see him pause before Arthur who, like the rest of us, has been knocking himself out snapping *tendus* dynamically to the side. Now the music stops too. We watch. Balanchine bends down and grabs Arthur's foot. With one hand around the ankle and the other grasping the instep, he stretches the foot, wiggles it up and down into a slightly more arched position. Then he lets go of the foot, straightens up, and takes a step back. He's still focused on Arthur.

"Point your toe." Arthur points real hard.

"Harder." Arthur outdoes himself.

"Ha-a-r-der!" demands the slavemaster. You can see the strain in Arthur's neck, he's pointing so hard. We are transfixed.

"HARDER!!" Says Mr. B/Simon Legree, loud and clear, "or I send you back to LITTLE ROCK!" Which he pronounces with the emphasis on "rock."

Arthur looks startled—we're all shocked—then his eyes light up and he grins. A flash of teeth. Arthur is a born New Yorker. He's never been near Little Rock. We break into smiles too, tension dissipated. The hazing is over. Arthur is baptized. He belongs. The congregation goes back to barre work. Mr. Balanchine looks smug. He's obviously pleased with his personal contribution to the Civil Rights struggle.

Balanchine assigned that pretty little Virginia Rich from Atlanta as Arthur's first on-stage partner. They'd already been "integrated" in classes at the School for quite a while, well ahead of the rest of the country, and Mr. B cunningly contrived to put together not only black and white, but North and South, when he chose Ginger as the first partner of the newly engaged dancer. Of course, at the time of Arthur's first company class, I, for one, had no idea of the ballet that was taking shape in Balanchine's mind—the ballet called *Agon.*

In classical Greek, the term includes a family of related meanings. Ἀγών denotes a "struggle" or athletic contest, such as that between wrestlers at the Olympic Games. It could refer to chariot races or foot races. It suggests any kind of competition, a political contest for example, or the fiercely fought-over award, among Athenians, for the coveted drama prize. It could mean an armed battle, and this military sense extends, according to the lexicon, to an action at law, a legal battle or trial. As with any conflict there is a prize at stake, some form of gain or loss.

What should be underscored here is that the word implies a *collective*, that is, a significant social presence. The primary meaning given for ἀγών in Liddell and Scott is that of an "assembly," the venue or arena where the contest may be observed. Perhaps more surprising, it includes the audience that assembles to observe the action. It might be a courtroom trial, a wrestling match, or a charged performance of *Antigone*, but the citizens who attend are considered to be active participants, not passive watchers. (Think of current-day basketball or baseball fans, racing buffs, the audience at a prize-fight.) For the Greeks, this potent context of community—the abiding civil presence—was not confined to sports or politics or courtroom proceedings. The principle springs from

Agon rehearsal (1957). Arthur Mitchell supporting Diana Adams in the pas de deux at the School of American Ballet's new studios on Broadway and 82nd Street. Photograph © Martha Swope.

the same civic impetus that prescribes the Chorus, the voice of the people, as a necessary component of tragic drama.

Agon was the third major collaboration between Stravinsky and Balanchine that sprang from a Greek theme. Within two years of that first company class, the great *pas de deux* Balanchine designed for Arthur Mitchell and Diana Adams would catapult the young black dancer into widespread recognition. For many he would become a living icon. He was not spared the slights, the humiliations, the refusals to serve blacks at restaurants, the treatment this nation for so long has accorded its darker-complexioned citizens. In time, however, Arthur would create many memorable roles; who can forget his "Puck" in *A Midsummer Night's Dream*? He would win the hearts of Russian audiences in St. Petersberg. And, like Balanchine, against all odds he would found a school and pioneer a vital, exciting company—The Dance Theatre of Harlem—an all-black ballet company that continues to thrive. He would eventually be honored at the Kennedy Center for his special contributions to dance and art—and the integrity of his goals.

Long after the premiere of *Agon*, Arthur commented to Francis Mason on Balanchine's use of skin tones in the *pas de deux*: "With Diana being so pale and me being so dark" he recalled, "even the placing of the hands or the arms provided a color structure integrated into the choreographic one."[2] But it was Melissa Hayden, another principal dancer in that explosive ballet, who brought back the vexed racial context of the period. The first time you saw Arthur and Diana doing the *pas de deux*, she pointed out, "it was really awesome to see a black hand touch a white skin. That's where we were coming from in the fifties."[3]

Among other wonders—and there are many things to marvel at in *Agon*—the ballet presented Balanchine's Alexandrian solution to the problem of racial discrimination. On his own territory, in the one arena where he had complete control, at the theater where an audience gathered to take part in a dramatic action, he publicly cut through the twisted knot of race relations. And Arthur had definitely arrived. He was in a class of his own.

18

Agon: Point Counterpoint

HE TRAIN IS EMERGING after mile upon oppressive mile
in the dark. In 1953, the tunnel under the Simplon Pass is
the longest rail tunnel in the world. NYCB is scattered throughout two or three cars of the Venice-Simplon Orient Express. This
is a branch of that most romantic of trains, the Orient Express beloved of Agatha Christie and Alfred Hitchcock, which runs all the
way south to Istanbul. We've been traveling north from Genoa to
our engagement in Munich and I know by the gradual, slightly
unsteady emergence into light that we've left Piedmont and Italy
behind and are headed into Switzerland. It's early November and
pretty cold. Mr. B, bracing himself against the wind, is standing on
the open platform at the back of the car when I step out for my first
unobstructed sight of the Alps. We watch white giants stride by.
Towers of snow and ice, the more distant peaks shrouded in mist.
The sky is overcast, a luminous light gray, and there's no sound
but the chugging of the train, the labored ascent.

We've had recent marriages in the company, divorces, annulments, remarriages, a pregnancy—and as the train chugs and jerks along I break the silence to ask Mr. Balanchine what he thinks. Can't a dancer be a dancer and also marry? maybe have children? He turns to look straight at me. "*Any* woman can have baby," he answers after a brief consideration. The disparaging tone is replaced by a statement of the obvious: "Not everybody can be dancer."

Skip forward four years to 1957. I've just turned twenty-six. It's November and pretty cold outside. Inside, in the dropped-level studio at the School of American Ballet's new quarters on Broadway and 83rd Street, Barbara Walczak and I are both perspiring and a little breathless. We've been doing all kinds of jumps and fast footwork, abrupt moves and sudden stops, mostly in unison, sometimes sequentially in *canon* mode. We're part of a threesome with Todd Bolender as the central figure, but now Todd is relaxing against the barre, hand on hip, and talking quietly with Diana Adams. At the piano is Kolya Kopeikine; Mr. Stravinsky is seated on the bench in front of the mirror wearing a sleeveless sweater over his shirt (he's used to California weather), and Mr. Balanchine is working with Basia and me on the Gailliard in *Agon*. Oh boy, is it complicated! Plus, there's not a lot of time to get everything absolutely right; the premiere is scheduled for the first of December, just a few weeks ahead. We've gone over the series of high leaps in unison that Edwin Denby called a "duet in the air, like flying twins (*haute danse*)" in his review.[1] We've completed the Gailliard with its curious ending of arm gestures set to total silence. Now we're waiting to see what Mr. B wants to do next. But Balanchine has turned to Stravinsky who is slowly shaking his head.

After the three opening dances that constitute Part I, the central portion of *Agon* (Part II) begins with two sets of dances that have courtly Renaissance names. After the Sarabande and the Gailliard of our *pas de trois*, there's a final Coda followed by the Bransle Simple, Bransle Gay, and Bransle Double danced by Melissa Hayden, with Roy Tobias and Jonathan Watts. This whole lively, quirky, difficult midsection concludes with the slow-motion, intricate, breath-taking *pas de deux* designed for Diana Adams and Arthur

Agon rehearsal (1957). Mr. B rehearses the Bransles: Roy Tobias kneeling, Jonathan Watts supporting Melissa Hayden. Seated on bench in front of mirror (left to right): Barbara Milberg, Barbara Walczak, Edith Brozak, Mr. B and Igor Stravinsky, Mme. Lucia Davidova, and Bernard Taper (biographer of Balanchine). Photograph © Martha Swope.

Mitchell. The only "baroque" thing about any of these dances, so far as I can make out, is their exuberant motion, their contrived irregularities, as of baroque pearls. How little they resembled the grave or gallant measures of the dances whose names they bore—even less, the simple configurations of the peasant round-dance in the case of the "Bransles."

In the Bransles, just as in the electric opening segment of *Agon*, Melissa Hayden's jazzy *élan*, the glitter of irony, her high-speed footwork, the dragonfly instantaneousness of her switches in direction, the spare angularity of her style, all contribute to a veritable restatement of the baroque. Were Stravinsky and Balanchine "deconstructing" the mode? creating an anti-baroque? a through-the-looking-glass baroque? Lacking any embellishment other than its intricate score and equally elaborate choreography, what remained of "baroque style" in the new ballet was its quality of peculiarity, of subtle distortion, of departure from the expected. Surely in these characteristics, and in the precarious intertwining of the classical and the contemporary, *Agon* carried the DNA of *Apollo*, the double helix of *Concerto Barocco*.

On this November day, Balanchine has been rehearsing the First Pas de Trois for Todd, Basia, and me. The Gailliard for the two women follows Todd's solo, a kooky Sarabande that exploits Bolender's personal idiom as effectively as did the "Phlegmatic" variation Balanchine devised for him years earlier in Hindemith's *Four Temperaments*. But this dance is exquisitely tailored to suit a cocky postmodern "attitude," not a medieval humour. Denby caught the flavor of it perfectly: "The boy, left alone, begins to walk a Sarabande, elaborately coiled and circumspect. It recalls court dance as much as a cubist still life recalls a pipe or guitar. . . . And the cool lift of his wrong-way-round steps and rhythms gives the nonsense so apt a turn people begin to giggle."[2] After Todd's Sarabande and our Gailliard comes the Coda in which all three of us dance together. "In triple canon" notes the sage of dance critics, "the dancers do idiotic slenderizing exercises, theoretically derived from court gesture, while the music foghorns in the fashion of musique concrète."

But in the space between our Gailliard and the Coda in which Todd will join our idiotic slenderizing exercises, something momentous is occurring. Balanchine had composed an unusual ending for the Gailliard: *nine* counts of arm gestures in dead silence. These arm movements indeed served as a bridge to the Coda, but also heralded a far more complex transition. Our series of silent

Walczak and Milberg rehearsing the Gailliard in *Agon*. In front of mirror: Mr. B with Stravinsky (standing), Mme. Davidova, and Bernard Taper. Photograph © Martha Swope.

gestures announced a sea change in the *score*, or as musicologist Charles M. Joseph put it, "a turn of historic proportions." Midway through the ballet, he points out, Stravinsky suddenly moves into "a full-blown Webernesque twelve-tone approach . . . first manifested in the coda of the First Pas de Trois." It marked the composer's "conversion to dodecaphony," comments Joseph, a sudden about-face that was "not only jolting" but "remarkably fresh and facile."[3]

Apparently, the uncharacteristic gestures-in-silence that Balanchine set for us at the close of the Gailliard articulate the exact moment in *Agon* at which this leap occurs. To put it another way, they mark the point at which a neoclassical, jazz-tinged, modernist composition loops like a Möbius Strip into postmodern serialism, with its twelve-tone rows, its "pitch sets," its mathematically calculated inversions and retrograde inversions. It was an ἀγών of modes.

Stravinsky, who had always positioned himself in fierce opposition to Schoenberg in the musical arena, became increasingly interested in twelve-tone compositional techniques at roughly the time of Schoenberg's death in 1951, at a point when he himself, it seems, was experiencing a species of "burn-out." After several years of intense study and application, the composer had grown adept in the development of serial techniques and by 1954, according to Joseph, he had composed much of the music for *Agon*.

It cannot be coincidence that in that very same year, in 1954, Stravinsky's most valued collaborator had chosen Schoenberg's *Opus 34* as the score for his new ballet. Balanchine had caused the same music to be played twice over; had conceived two entirely different ways to choreograph it. Clearly, Balanchine had also studied and applied himself to a Schoenberg score in every detail. He had experimented, worked his way through a twelve-tone composition to the point where he could confidently create "a powerful and a paradoxical ballet," as Denby put it. By 1957, when Stravinsky had stunningly integrated the warring musical modes in *Agon*, Balanchine was alert to the jointure. He would splice neoclassical and serial idioms seamlessly together, just as the score demanded. *But* he would take a moment—just nine heartbeats—to indicate the precise point at which time-honored old compositional methods corkscrewed into new machine-age techniques. There would be a "liminal zone." A space of sacred silence to mark that a passage is in progress, a significant transition is taking place—preceded and followed by ritual clowning.

This is what I remember. Balanchine had finished teaching Basia and me the Gailliard a few days earlier, with a momentary hesitation at the end. He'd assumed a kind of cramped position and stared at the floor for a while. When he let us go, I had the

Mr. B and Stravinsky with Kolya Kopeikine at the piano during *Agon* rehearsal. Seated on bench: Edward Bigelow (profile) and Ann Hutchinson, Laban dance notation specialist. Photo © Martha Swope.

impression that there was something still to be added, something he was not quite ready to set. Maybe Walczak had the same feeling. But the next time we meet for rehearsal the uncertainty is gone. Balanchine now appears energized, alive; his manner businesslike. You know he knows what he's going to do. At the end of the Gailliard he places Basia and me close together, both of us bent motionless in a "freeze frame." He points us in the same direction, canted forward and turned about forty-five degrees toward

Walczak, Bolender, and Milberg rehearsing the Coda in *Agon.* Seated in front of mirror: Ann Hutchinson recording the movements, Mr. B with Stravinsky, Mme. Davidova. Photograph © Martha Swope.

stage right, but not in exactly parallel poses. Now Mr. B counts out nine counts in the exact same rhythm we'd previously been moving to. He beats time up and down with one hand, as if conducting, thumb and index finger forming a little circle, each quietly spoken count accompanied by the slightest nod. Finally, he indicates that without changing our position we are to fill the counts with arm movements. *Nothing* is to move but our arms. We are to invent the movements ourselves (he gives us a general idea). They are to be angular, abrupt rather than graceful, and absolutely precise in tempo.

Basia and I follow Balanchine's instructions carefully, imitate his static, slightly crouched pose and move our arms around. We look like a pair of grasshoppers marking time. Nine counts, four hands—silently concluding a 9/4 rhythmic set. In the silence that follows the cessation of the music, the motions of our four hands project a kind of contrapuntal groping in the vacuum. It is this ending-after-the-ending that has made Stravinsky frown and slowly shake his head as he sits watching on the bench.

I'm just a bit distracted. I've been paying careful attention, listening and doing everything Mr. B is telling us to do, but one part of me is constantly directed toward the shiny new wedding band on my left hand. I keep catching glimpses of it. It feels strange. I've never worn a ring in my life and I'm thinking *you don't wear a ring onstage.* I remember how Ruthie Sobotka persuaded Kubrick to give her the thinnest gold band possible—she showed it to us in the dressing room—and she covered it with greasepaint and powder at each performance so it wouldn't be seen. Mine is heavy, a thick beaten-gold ring—should I remove it when I perform? Would that constitute a breach of the marriage vows? A symbolic denial, of sorts? Ruthie and "Cupcake" were splitting up. But I must be professional: this is my work, my career.

I snap out of it, realize that Balanchine and Stravinsky are in the midst of a heated argument. Stravinsky is shaking his head, Balanchine is gesticulating. They've gone back to Russian. Intense debate. Finally the older man gives the least little shrug, raises his hands from his lap, just a couple of inches with the palms facing, then lets them drop back to his thighs. He's not convinced, it seems to say, but he won't argue any more. Mr. B returns to Basia and me: Okay, it's in. Now it's Todd's turn to join us and we begin to dance as a threesome. What were they arguing about? Did the nine extra counts interfere with Stravinsky's per-second-per-second timing? (Joseph mentions that Stravinsky had fastidiously marked the duration of individual passages *in total seconds* [my italics], "sometimes as often as every few measures" and, with Balanchine, had timed *Agon* very carefully to last a scant twenty minutes.)[4] But Mr. Stravinsky looks interested now; he's absorbed in the serial intricacies of the Coda, and I forget I'm wearing a ring that's not quite three months old.

We were married in Evanston at the end of August 1957, though we'd met two years earlier over a bridge game at his apartment in

Chicago. Bid and made a grand slam in diamonds. Mickey loved the ballet, had attractive manners and a prep school education; he worked at a Chicago printing firm and ushered at the Opera House when there was something he wanted to see. He owned a cute little British sports car—a black two-seater MG-TC with the steering wheel on the right—and had come to Chicago to study at the Academy of Design. He seemed to know everything there was to know about painting and architecture and graphic design. What books to read. With pale skin, dark eyes, and thick glossy black hair, he looked very like a French movie star. *And,* when we returned to Chicago for a short season in the spring of 1957, I discovered that we both had the same gorgeous recording by tenor Hugues Cuenod of sixteenth- and seventeenth-century Spanish and Italian songs. I put a horrendous scratch in his record when I tried to lift the tone arm off the disk, which is how we ended up married. Full of remorse—and hope—I mailed him a replacement from New York, along with a photograph (a glamorous glossy head shot) and a note, and he responded by asking me to come back to Chicago for July and August. He'd intelligently arranged a job for me with a friend, Eric Braun, who was engaging dancers for the summer festival in nearby Ravinnia.

So I flew out and spent the summer with Mickey, except when I was one of the peasants in a Breughel painting come suddenly alive. He taught me how to read a road map, to navigate for a "rally," and how to do a "racing downshift" using the engine to slow the car instead of the brakes. He could "drift" the little MG around corners. He took me to a café on the South Side where they had really good spare ribs and Michelob beer on tap. He was terrific at crosswords. We did quarrel over the pronunciation of the word spelled "m-i-s-l-e-d." He mistakenly insisted it was "mizzled" while I championed "my-zilled." But it wasn't until he pulled the TC over to the edge of a grassy space, bent down, and plucked me a daisy, that I decided to hook up with this guy. He elected to return East when I told him the New York season was pending, and we called our parents, in tandem, to tell them we were planning to marry almost immediately. I figured *my* mother would be relieved. I'd gone over the quarter-century mark. Didn't know what *his* mom would say.

He calls first, to Greenwich, Connecticut. "Hello, Mother? It's me. I wanted to let you know that Barbara and I are getting married. (Silence.) Yes, you met her. (Silence.) **Barbara. Milberg.** At Aunt Dossie's, when you visited." She hangs up. Oh dear. I'd met Sally and Howard Jr. in Ohio at her sister's house and we'd played bridge. I shouldn't have said the F-word when I missed that trick. Well, she'd made her point.

Next, I call my mom upstate in New York, the area in the Catskill Mountains known as the "Borscht Circuit." Good news, I tell her, I'm getting married. In a couple of days. Yes, right here in Chicago. No, I don't want to wait. No, I don't want a big wedding. No, the date is set. A Justice of the Peace. It'll be simpler that way. After a long moment she asks three questions:

"What does he look like?"
"Oh, he's really good-looking! Dark hair, dark eyes, very
    nice!" (I don't tell her how nice he smells.)
"Um-hmh. What's his name?" (Here it comes!)
"Howard Shreve Fisher . . . the Third." A long pause.
"Is he *Jewish?*"
"No, mom." A *very* long pause.
(Brightly): "Oh well . . . with a name like *Fisher* we don't
    have to tell *every*body!"

Point, counterpoint.

After the ceremony in Evanston, where the blessed Vida Brown suddenly materialized and metamorphosed from my Ballet Mistress into my Matron of Honor, Mickey and I drove from Chicago to New York without stopping except for food and gas. It was the end of August and hot, hot, hot. We traveled light, with the top down most of the way, both my legs dangling over the side. Dumped our stuff in the same West 78th Street apartment where Tanny and Balanchine had shared that home-cooked, slightly tipsy Chinese dinner, visited with both sets of parents—and decided to go see Mr. B. Then we'd honeymoon, in September, at his grand-mother's farmhouse in Maine.

Balanchine was in Connecticut. We drove out to his place, where Eddie Bigelow was keeping him company. Tanny was away, with her mother I think, undergoing a course of therapy. Mr. B looked inquisitively at Mickey, then walked over to the refrigerator and withdrew a bottle of vodka. It had a large spray of tarragon from the garden floating in it. He politely congratulated us on the marriage. Nobody was in a talkative mood, though, and after the hospitable drink we thanked Mr. B and took off. "We've seen a beautiful man," said my new husband as he turned out of the driveway, "Now I'm going to show you a beautiful house." He drove us the short distance to the Philip Johnson house, a circular glass structure on a Connecticut hillside thick with birches, with its adjacent non-see-through guest house which, like the third little pig's, was built all of brick. Contrapuntal architecture.

Balanchine had been away from the company for nearly a year. In 1956, he'd sustained two major blows in swift succession. Arlene Croce gives a succinct account in "The Spelling of Agon" as part of the history leading directly to that ballet: "On October 2, 1956, Stravinsky had a major stroke while conducting in Berlin. New York City Ballet had just completed its season there the night before. Balanchine took the news hard. Betty Cage, NYCB's general manager, recalls hearing muffled sobs outside the hotel room where she had set up her office in Berlin. Opening the door, she found Balanchine, too overcome to tell her what had happened. Robert Craft reports that when Stravinsky left the hospital, five weeks later, the doctor was saying that he had not more than six months to live." Meanwhile, Croce goes on, "Tanaquil Le Clercq, Balanchine's wife and one of his principal ballerinas, lay ill, unable to dance. She had been stricken on October 31st in Copenhagen, the next to last stop on the European tour. The doctors diagnosed polio. Balanchine was in a state of collapse."[5]

The company fulfilled its 1956/1957 engagements as scheduled, but without Mr. B. We had a twelve-week winter season at the City Center, three weeks at the Chicago Opera House the following spring, and then we were pretty much at loose ends until November of 1957. We weren't exactly drifting but we'd lost impetus. We weren't exactly somber but the general mood was far from sparkling. During performances, the downstage right wing was never empty, but Mr. B wasn't in it; an almost palpable absence. We took company class during our engagements, we were carefully rehearsed, but everything had a faint whiff of ashes. The news from Warm Springs was not even lukewarm: Although Tanny had recovered partial use of one arm, she would probably never be able to walk. Stravinsky was seriously ill.

In the fall of 1957 everything is suddenly utterly changed. Stravinsky has made a miraculous recovery. Tanny is not only alive but slowly gaining ground. Mr. Balanchine is back—supercharged. He's consulting with Stravinsky on the new ballet, he's scheduling rehearsals, he's all over the place! Energy pours in. The nest of ashes is exploding into flame.

Agon was a singularity. An unpredictable big bang that sped out of the dark, illuminated the moment, and sped enlarging into the darkness ahead. It was not like any ballet we'd ever done before. The nine counts that Mr. B added at the close of the Gailliard—the silent counts that had Stravinsky shaking his head—were eventually expunged from the work. They were never added to the score. But I like to imagine that, at the time he was composing the ballet, Balanchine had compressed a momentous transfiguration into our "freeze frame." What you saw were two people struck motionless, unable to move anything but their upper limbs. Like infants waving their arms meaninglessly, in awkward motion. Like people who have undergone a severe stroke. Like individuals suddenly paralyzed. Then, after the instant of stasis, the figures were moving again, dancing "full out," but in an entirely new mode.

Stravinsky and Balanchine's deliberate crossover, in *Agon*, into mathematically controlled music and movement echoes a much earlier, monumental, break from established codes. The poet Alighieri's move from Latin into the vernacular, at the turn of the fourteenth century, marks that point at which medieval culture and aesthetic conventions crossed over a liminal zone to become

Early Renaissance thought and art. Dante sparked his revolution, not in the *Commedia* (or "Divine Comedy") but earlier in the *Vita Nuova* with the Latin phrase *Incipit vita nova* ("here begins the new life") which he set at the close of its opening sentence. This ending phrase, seamlessly joining the conventional Latin to the living Italian in which the book was written, promised a new literary life to the vernacular. Dante boldly cast this remarkable collection of sonnets, meditations, and visions in his native tongue, in the "sweet new style," and *La Vita Nuova*, the vernacular form, not the Latin, has remained its title. In its own quiet way, the nine measures of loaded silence that Balanchine inserted between the Gailliard and the Coda of *Agon* signified more than a personal recovery, more than a return to art and life. Those nine counts signaled a quantum leap into a new universe, a realm of technological sophistication without precedent.

The ballet as a whole executed a bold Dantean leap. I do not know whether Mr. Balanchine or Mr. Stravinsky were familiar with the works of Osip Mandelstam—close contemporary of Boris Pasternak and Anna Akhmatova—the poet who was sent into exile and an early death for his anti-Stalinist convictions. Yet the curious choice of *Agon*, or "struggle," for the title of their ballet brings the great Russian poet to the forefront and suggests its significance. For me, it places an American ballet in a direct line from the Russian masters to the Italian master to the wrestling matches of classical Greece. In "Conversation about Dante," (Razgovor o Dante), Mandelstam singles out Dante's "naked and gleaming wrestlers who walk about pluming themselves on their physical prowess before grappling in the decisive fight" (*Inferno*, XVI. 22–24), and styles the poet of the *Commedia* a "strategist of transformations and crossbreedings." Mandelstam's comment on the Dantean scene of struggle might easily underlie Balanchine and Stravinsky's conception of *Agon*: "The wrestlers winding themselves into a tangle in the arena may be regarded as an example of a transformation of instruments and a harmony."[6]

Agon was the phoenix nest bursting into flame. Out of it came new life, new invention, a new Firebird for a new time. It was not

Apollonian; it was not Orphic. Croce framed its essence in the starkest, most vivid terms: "*Agon*, as Balanchine choreographed it, had an atomic-age urgency; it had thrills, danger, apocalyptic energy. And it was wall-to-wall dancing, without even the shadowy pretext of a competition before the gods."[7]

Two Russian geniuses had designed a muscular, vigorous, acrobatic, elegant, compact, contrapuntal, and marvelously healthy bird of fire. A kind of flaming two-headed American eagle. They had come back together, resurrected from disease and disaster and near death. Each had returned from a personal ἀγών in that lethal shadow zone. Like Dante who agonized in his own hell of exile, and like the later Irish poet who could not separate the dancer from the dance, these two had shaped a living work of art out of tragic joy. Point, counterpoint.

Epilogue

Our revels now are ended

HE LAST CLASS I taught at City College was a graduate English seminar in seventeenth-century poetry and prose. I had designed the course to approach the period as an "age of exploration," both global and intellectual. Along with poetry, essays, and one singularly befitting play, I'd assigned readings that would suggest the scope and excitement of the travels, the dangerous sea voyages, the discoveries in that "brave new world" of unknown plants, native tribes, alien customs. We examined the incendiary impact of Galileo's new physics, the Copernican "heresy" that removed our planet from the center of the universe, the swift advances in mathematics that were disturbing theologians.

Some of our readings illuminated religious conflicts and the political arena, for this was a period in English history that included a nearly successful attempt by religious extremists to blow up the entire government, a regicide, a troubled parliamentary interregnum, and a return to the monarchy. Not by chance, the mid-seventeenth century saw the publication of a pragmatic—almost Machiavellian—new political philosophy. Hobbes's *Leviathan* was, in essence, a survival manual for civil societies subject to terrorist attack. This was the fall semester of 2002, just one year after religious extremists had reduced a sizable chunk of downtown Manhattan to ashes, its buildings to grotesque metal skeletons, and these studies had more than a theoretical significance to students at the City College of New York.

It was a tough course and well attended. We'd met once a week for nearly two hours from the beginning of September to the middle of December, with additional hours scheduled for office conferences. I was about to retire and had planned a little celebration for our final meeting. I got to school early that afternoon, and when the students arrived they found cookies and chips and various drinks on a side table under the chalkboard. Opposite the board was a window that spanned the length of the room with its long seminar table and surrounding chairs. We were on the sixth floor of the building that housed Humanities, and the view ranged west over buildings pink in the sunset to the Hudson River and the Jersey cliffs beyond. Upriver you could just make out the George Washington Bridge. Final papers were not due until the following week, and we were devoting this last session to what was announced somewhat enigmatically on the syllabus as "Memory Lane." The door to the room was closed. This was a strictly private affair.

A few weeks earlier, in place of an in-class written exam, I'd asked the kids to memorize something from among the works we'd read. Something that had appealed to them. It could be poetry (minimum of eight lines of verse) or a prose passage. They were to recite the lines aloud at the last class and say why they had chosen that particular selection. I told them that I, too, would try to memorize something from scratch and added that they might have to help me out. The "stickum" in their young brains was better than mine, I reminded them. On the other hand, I already knew what passage I wanted to commit to memory.

Along with the Cavalier and Metaphysical poets, essays by Bacon, Milton's impassioned argument against censorship, and Thomas Hobbes's dark construct of the natural order, we'd read *The Tempest*—Shakespeare's last play before retiring from the theater.[1] The passage I had in mind was the magician Prospero's speech in Act 4, the lines that some scholars believe to be Shakespeare's own farewell to his art. For me, the passage carried a double significance. Not only was this to be my final class, but Prospero's speech invariably summoned up another magician from out of my past, partly because of its theatrical context but more forcibly for its elegiac power, its aura of impending loss.

Perhaps more than anyone, Balanchine knew that ballet is a fragile art. For me, the passage brought back Mr. B's repeated assertion that after he was gone his works would cease to exist as such, would vanish as it were into thin air. I didn't know at the time that Balanchine was not only familiar with *The Tempest*, but that he'd worked with Margaret Webster on a Broadway production of the play in 1945, the year before he invited me to join Ballet Society. He'd been asked to choreograph the movements for Ariel, the beloved sprite Prospero holds in bondage. He staged the sequences for that enchanting creature of air, who is reluctantly freed in the last act shortly after Prospero forswears his magic arts, breaks his wand in two, buries it "certain fathoms in the earth" and "drowns" his book of spells in the sea.

On this late December afternoon I rose first, waited for quiet—silently invoked the Mother of the Muses—and spoke the lines. Miraculously, without a single lapse or falter, out came the cadenced phrases of Prospero's grand farewell to the realms of illusion. He is preparing to leave behind the intricate scenarios of magic, to return home. The *masque*, the classical spectacle he has wrought upon this primitive island with Ariel's help, is concluded. The ballet is over, the masquers have disappeared. Now, in his double identity as wizard and exiled Duke of Milan, he addresses Ferdinand, his daughter's suitor. That is, he speaks to the younger generation, perhaps to all the generations that will come after:

> Our revels now are ended. These our actors,
> As I foretold you, were all spirits and
> Are melted into air, into thin air;
> And—like the baseless fabric of this vision—
> The cloud-capped towers, the gorgeous palaces,
> The solemn temples, the great globe itself,
> Yea, all which it inherit, shall dissolve,
> And like this insubstantial pageant faded,
> Leave not a rack behind. We are such stuff
> As dreams are made on, and our little life
> Is rounded with a sleep. Sir, I am vexed;
> Bear with my weakness; my old brain is troubled.[2]

I have to admit I was pleased. It set off a series of genuinely in-spired recitations. As the sky darkened, students stood up Quaker-fashion, as the spirit moved them, and each in turn explained why Ben Jonson's elegy for his dead child, or Donne's holy sonnet, or Herrick's brazen mistress, or Marlowe's seductive shepherd, or Bacon's ironic take on Truth, or Katherine Philip's disdainful view of "the married state," had appealed to the imagination, mind, or gut. One young woman announced with becoming transparency that she had chosen her selection because it was the shortest she could find and easy to remember. And to everyone's surprise, a good-looking young fellow who had been one of the quieter stu-dents performed an astonishing feat of memory *plus* delivering a highly entertaining reading. He wrote to me later: "I hope you will forgive my outburst of acting in our last class. I used to make my living at it, but have been in semi-retirement since the birth of my son and most of the acting I do is of the Dr. Seuss and Curious George variety, when I read to my son before bed. And, dork that I am, I leapt at the chance to say someone else's words in a roomful of people." Dork? All in all, it was a trip!

From dumb dancer to tenured full professor, from the premiere of *Agon* in 1957 to graduate English in 2002 was a more compli-cated trip in time. *But how the hell did I end up in the seventeenth century?*

I lost touch. First with the dancers and staff of my original company, then more and more completely with the world of dance that had been my life. In 1958, the year after my marriage, Jerry Robbins invited me to join his newly formed Ballets: USA. It was an unexpected piece of kindness. New York City Ballet was planning a long tour that began in Japan and ended in Australia, and although both Mickey and I were dying to go, the company could not find a place for my new husband in any capacity. So I joined Jerry's small troupe as one of its principal dancers. We opened Gian-Carlo Menotti's newly organized "Festival of Two Worlds" in Spoleto that year, and my husband traveled with us. We rented a little Fiat 500, and on days we weren't rehearsing or performing made side trips to Perugia, Assisi, and Rome. We toiled up the Umbrian hills with their narrow winding roads, beehive-shaped haystacks in every field; shot back from the capital along the straight Roman road. Along with Ben Shahn, conductor Thomas Shippers, and other well-known artists and musicians, Alexander Calder was in Spoleto for the opening of the festival that year. The maker of elegant mobiles liked Mickey, who had attended the Art Institute in Chicago and spoke his language. This was a godsend. Sandy spent time with my new husband while the company was rehearsing; he took the newlyweds under his wing and told us good places to eat when we got to Paris. We had a kind of extended honeymoon that summer, but although we did travel to Europe together later, it was the only time my husband accompanied me on tour; he had his own work to do.

In Jerry's company our accommodations and means of travel were modest. I remember one very bumpy bus trip in the Dolomites the following year, when Werner Torkanovsky, our conductor, suddenly sprang into the aisle, pulled out a tiny one-stringed fiddle (a native instrument called a *goosla*), and began wildly bowing the Mendelssohn Violin Concerto. As we veered around curves Werner was tossed from side to side, while at every major bump the bridge of the instrument collapsed. We shrieked with laughter.

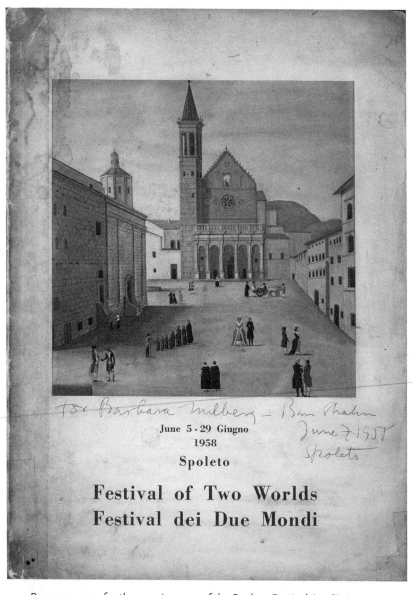

For Barbara Milberg — Ben Shahn

June 7 1958
Spoleto

June 5 - 29 Giugno
1958

Spoleto

Festival of Two Worlds
Festival dei Due Mondi

Program cover for the opening year of the Spoleto Festival (1958). Inscription by painter Ben Shahn. Author's collection.

Costume party for Jerome Robbins's Ballets: USA in Spoleto, Italy (June 1958). Howard Fisher ("Mickey") with umbrella, Bob Bakanak and Richard Bachrach (dancer Beryl Towbin's husband) behind Milberg (crouching, in striped shirt), principal dancer Erin Martin in fluffy white wig, and a garlanded musician. Jerry in shadow (far right foreground) facing dancers, as Wolf Man in fur hat and huge fur mittens. Photographer unknown, author's collection.

Ballets: USA performed in places I'd never been before: Belgrade, Dubrovnik, Tel Aviv, Athens, Madrid. Flying from Belgrade to Dubrovnik, our Russian-built two-engine plane circled a pasture on the side of a mountain, then landed. We watched, hardly daring to breathe, as a disgruntled shepherd moved his flock away from the plane's path. There was no airfield. Dubrovnik is a beautiful

Mickey Fisher and me (in hat) with Morelli family, whose apartment we shared (Spoleto 1958). Mama and Papa Morelli flanking me; Mickey (above) with daughter Giuliana (right) and cousin. Photographer unknown, author's collection.

ancient city on the Adriatic coast. Above the town is a stone fortress perched on a cliff wet with sea-spray where *Hamlet* was performed for summer tourists. Great for drama, but it was no place for ballet. Fortunately, the U.S. military had built a sturdy wooden platform in the center of the town square for us. If I remember rightly, that's where Johnnie Jones and I danced *Afternoon of a Faun* together for the first time.

I toured intermittently with Jerry's company for five years. Aside from the birth of my daughter (the boys came later), two things stand out sharply in my memory: an encounter with poet and novelist Robert Graves near the beginning, and performing at the Kennedy White House near the end.

John Jones and Barbara Milberg in Robbins's *Afternoon of a Faun*, Dubrovnik, Yugoslavia (1959). Photo: Richard Evans, Stage Manager of Ballets: USA.

Afternoon of a Faun, Dubrovnik (1959). Photo: Richard Evans.

I came to meet Robert Graves through a fluke. A pleasant well-spoken Englishwoman had opened Spoleto's first after-the-performance theatre club in 1959, the second year of the Festival. Everyone went to Jenny Cross's place after work to eat, wind down, and listen to blues. When Ballets: USA completed its weeks in Spoleto, Jenny, who was separated from her husband, traveled with us for part of the time. She was subject to really bad headaches and I was good at massaging them away, so we'd struck up a friendship. In the late summer of 1959, she introduced me to her father in the middle of London Airport just as we learned that one of our two small planes had gone down in the Ionian Sea.

We were flying from Athens to Edinburgh and had seen most of our personal trunks loaded onto one of the planes. As it turned out, the plane whose engine failed went down with all our costumes, the P.A. system, and two costly Byzantine icons that Jerry had acquired; most of our personal trunks were safe and the pilot had been able to swim to a nearby island. Within seconds after the news came over the loudspeakers, I saw a thick cluster of people surrounding someone at the center of the hall dissipate. Jenny took me by the arm and led me up to the solitary remaining figure, saying that she wanted me to meet her father. "Father, this is Barbara Milberg. She's read all your novels except *Antigua Penny Puce*" (out of print), "even *King Jesus*." My jaw dropped. So that's who her father was! Then she too shot off. I found myself alone with Robert Graves without a clue what to say. Speechless.

He was not the stooped, elderly scholar I'd envisioned. The learned writer who made ancient myths come alive. I was confronting a tall robust-looking man with ruddy cheeks and a tweed hat. All I could think of was the cover blurb on one of his books which stated that Robert Graves "worshiped the Triple Goddess." So I blurted out a question. Did he *really* believe in the Triple Goddess? He stared. Very blue eyes. I don't really remember what he answered. I vaguely recall a bit of levity, something about the Archbishop of Canterbury having hidden "every copy of *King Jesus* he could lay hands on *under his bed*." Her father, Jenny said when I found her again, had come to London from Majorca for prostate surgery and would be in hospital for several weeks. She had come to be with him, and remained behind when the company took off for Scotland.

After Edinburgh, where we performed in practice clothes, we opened in London. There were brand new costumes for opening night, and I was presented with a very large bouquet on stage. It was wrapped in cellophane and had a little envelope attached. I opened it in the dressing room and found a note: *"If you dance very well tonight,"* ran the inscription on the card, *"I shall believe in the goddess . . . love, Robert."* It was dated September 1959. You gotta hand it to a guy who sends you a note like that! I picked up Graves's newly reprinted *The White Goddess* at Faber & Faber's book store, took it to St. Thomas's Hospital, and asked the recovering author to sign it. Would I have raced through his novels, I wonder, if Mr. B had not encouraged me at a crucial moment to read *anything* I liked, so long as it "gives pleasure"?

Performing Robbins's *Opus Jazz* at Alvin Theatre (September 1958). Milberg (center) in white sweat shirt. Author's collection.

Alexandra, the first of my three children, was born in August 1961, at Flower Fifth Avenue Hospital. Jerry sent a postcard from Stonehenge, congratulating me on the birth and asking if I'd be ready to dance in the coming New York season. (Twenty-three years later, I received a phone call that sounded as if it had originated in another galaxy. *"Hi mom"* said a ghostly voice through heavy crackling and interference, *"Guess where I am."* I gave up. *"I'm calling from Stonehenge!"* My daughter had made her pilgrimage to the stone circle with a tour group, and they were preparing to leave. *"I've gotta hang up now"*—and the spectral visitation from prehistory was gone.) I danced in the October season but barely made it into my costumes. And the muscles for jumping . . . forget jumping!

On April 11, 1962, the dancers in Ballets: USA were flown into Washington aboard Air Force 1 at the request of the First Lady and President Kennedy. That evening we became the first ballet company ever to perform at the White House. We danced *Opus Jazz* (in sneakers) and *Afternoon of a Faun* (not in sneakers) in the East Wing before the Kennedys, the Shahinshah and Empress of

Ballets: USA production of Robbins's *The Concert* at the Alvin Theatre, Broadway (September 1958). Milberg (far left) as Mad Ballerina, Muriel Bentley in feather headpiece, Gwen Lewis (face covered), Pat Dunn (at right) with James Moore, and Tom Abbott seated behind them. Photographer unknown, author's collection.

Iran, and assorted dignitaries. In the photograph they sent me, now rather faded, Farah is wearing white lace and a tiara, Jackie a pink satin evening gown, and the President is shaking my hand—though all you can see of him is his collar and the side of his head. Jerry had been invited to the "small" dinner before the show. The rest of us were guided downstairs to the Men's and Ladies' Rooms where our costumes were hanging, and politely advised that these were our dressing rooms. We were offered the same New York State champagne that Jerry was drinking upstairs with the Kennedys, but he didn't have to dance. I will admit that none of us were exactly awestruck by our tenure in the White House bathrooms, but they did fly us back to New York City on Air Force 1. Except for a one-night stand at Madison Square Garden, where we danced in celebration of the President's birthday—and strained to catch a glimpse of Marilyn Monroe who was singing a throaty "Happy Birthday to You!" in a glittering red diva-gown—that was my last performance as a dancer: May 19, 1962. Benji was born exactly one year and three days after that birthday celebration, Sam five years

THE NEW YORK TIMES, SUNDAY, NOVEMBER 29, 1959.   **RADIO**   X 13

"BALLETS: U. S. A."—Jerome Robbins rehearses some members of his dance ensemble for a number to be seen during tonight's "Ed Sullivan Show." The program will be presented over the C.B.S. television network at 8 P. M.

Members of Ballets: USA rehearsing for *The Ed Sullivan Show*. Jerry (crouching in center), Erin Martin (far left), Johnny Jones and Milberg standing behind Robbins. Photo: Irving Haberman, *New York Times* clipping (11/29/59) from author's album.

later. You're swept into another life remote from theater. You lose touch.

I guess I ended up in the seventeenth century, that last course I taught at CCNY, because I loved it. Among the three periods of English literature I chose as my concentration in graduate studies—modern British and American poetry, seventeenth-century poetry and prose, and Victorian literature—the seventeenth century was closest to my heart. It wasn't my major. I'd been seduced by the poetry of Wallace Stevens, the American Modernist who became the subject of my doctoral dissertation, so Donne and Herbert, Milton, Marvell, and the Elizabethans were forced into second place. In the summer of 1970, I'd applied to City College as a freshman during Open Admissions: no tuition fees and it was close to home. The following year I was accepted into the Honors Program and offered a four-year B.A./M.A. course of study. By the junior year I was deep into English lit and classical mythology, had a minor in philosophy, and had taken my "physics for poets" (light on the math) to satisfy the core requirement. And I was beginning to read Greek. I was a good student. Not only was I insatiably curious and a sucker for research, but the discipline I'd learned at ballet school and in theater transferred easily to studies. I never submitted a paper after the deadline. Like every other performer, I didn't have to be told twice to get on stage on time. When the curtain goes up you better be there.

I have a vivid memory of bringing one of my professors backstage, at Lincoln Center, to meet Mr. Balanchine. Eddie Bigelow kindly arranged the entry from the house to the stage immediately after the performance. I headed for the downstage right wing like a homing pigeon and there stood Mr. B, as always. But older, his hair almost white, the shape thicker, his face lined. I knew he'd had a heart bypass. When he hugged me I nearly wept. This man, I suddenly understood, had taught me more than anybody else ever would. After the introductions, Balanchine asked what I was studying. I told him, and added that I was heading for a doctorate. He drew himself up at that point and announced "I am already doctor!" Universities kept conferring degrees on him, he said; he had more doctorates than he could count. I got the message that he was not particularly impressed by academic honors, but I also remember how his eyes lit up when I said I was learning to read classical Greek. Can you write it? I'm learning, I responded. Nodding energetically, he exclaimed "That's good!"

I didn't admit that I was practicing the script by writing my market lists in Greek. As it happens, the Greek alphabet lacked a few of the sounds I needed. Eggs, milk, hamburger, honey, and

Figaro cat food were okay ("Brillo" was a shoo-in) but mushrooms, Jello, and chips presented problems. I wonder, though. Would I have hit upon practicing Greek in the kitchen if Mr. B hadn't urged us to practice our *tendus* while washing up the dishes? Or standing at the stove?

Neither did I tell Mr. Balanchine that there was something about Wallace Stevens' poetry that reminded me of his choreography. Stevens once wrote *All poetry is experimental poetry* and Balanchine illustrated the aphorism not only with experimental ballets and new-invented movement, but in shaping dance for movies and television, the new media. I knew they were both originators, prime movers in their fields. They both possessed enormous *élan*, and both held to a remarkable economy—not a phrase more than needed, nor an unnecessary step. Their constructs could be spare or elaborate, the mood erotic, comic, mystical, or meditative. Both had a feel for design and were effortlessly musical. Both were unpredictable; each enjoyed a quirky sense of humor, and both the poet and the choreographer were pragmatists.

You don't want to stretch it too far. Stevens stood an imposing six feet, three inches tall, weighed some 255 pounds, wore size eleven and a half shoes and, like composer Charles Ives, spent most of his working life in New England in the insurance business. I felt that Balanchine was the greater phenomenon, possessed the greater wealth of invention, but I also knew that my slender, foxy choreographer and my poet both found their inspiration in the feminine. Balanchine, from the beginning, celebrated his own muses. Stevens invoked the One of Fictive Music, "Sister and mother and diviner love," and that fertile Green Queen whose "green mind made the world around her green." One of his greatest poems brought into being the nameless solitary woman who, striding along the beach at Key West, "sang beyond the genius of the sea":

> For she was the maker of the song she sang.
> The ever-hooded, tragic-gestured sea
> Was merely a place by which she walked to sing.[3]

Each was capable of elegant articulation and the beauty that attends precision. Above all, I knew that Stevens's theory of poetry could easily serve as Balanchine's *ars poetica* for choreography: *It must be abstract; It must change; It must give pleasure.* It must give pleasure. I remember Mr. B teasing me once, when the Tchaikovsky *Theme and Variations* had its premiere, in November 1947, and I'd asked him what the ballet "was about." This was the original ABT production set for Alicia Alonso and Igor Youskevitch at the old Metropolitan Opera House. Barbara Walczak and I had standing-room tickets, and from the rear of the orchestra watched the rival company perform its first Balanchine ballet with grace, dignity, and *bravura*. It received an enthusiastic reception. During curtain calls we both felt a hand grasp a shoulder, and whipped around to find Mr. B looking right in our faces. He appeared unusually pleased with himself, and approachable, so I asked him what the ballet "meant." Oh-h-h, he answered slowly in a sing-song nasal drawl, "I just want curtain to go up and everybody should be *happy!*"

Balanchine paid homage to Shakespeare with his vivid staging of *A Midsummer Night's Dream*. But looking back, it seems to me that the man himself was a figure straight out of *The Tempest*—a combination of impish Ariel and Prospero, the magus. In a recent *New Yorker* article, dance critic Joan Acocella tellingly described Balanchine's art as "the conjuring of extreme and secret states of the soul via ballet alone."[4] Wallace Stevens weighed over 250 pounds, but one of his very last poems, "The Planet on the Table," conjures up Ariel—the airy sprite who can appear in an instant and disappear just as quickly—as his poetic persona. For me, this late poem, this meditation on his life's work, speaks elegiacally for both artists. It begins simply:

> Ariel was glad he had written his poems.
> They were of a remembered time
> Or of something seen that he liked.

A bit further on, the words again seem to speak for both men:

Commencement exercises at the Graduate School and University Center of CUNY (Spring 1980). Milberg, in doctoral robes, is "hooded" by Dr. Arnold Proshansky, Executive Director. Robbins, about to receive an honorary doctorate, is seated at far right. Snapshot by neighbor Esther Schmulewicz, author's collection.

It was not important that they survive.
What mattered was that they should bear
Some lineament or character,
Some affluence, if only half-perceived,
In the poverty of their words,
Of the planet of which they were part.[5]

With a lot of help, I made it through the B.A./M.A. course of study, continued at the Graduate School of City University and received my doctorate in 1980, just when every opening for English instructors was answered by literally hundreds of hopefuls. There were virtually no jobs. At the commencement exercises, however, I was startled to read in the program that one of the honorary doctorates to be awarded that day would go to Jerome Robbins in recognition of his distinguished service to the City of New York. Sure enough, there sat Jerry on the raised area with the other honorees, in robe and mortarboard, and a short gray beard, his eyes focused meditatively on the floor. After I was "hooded," I walked over to the raised section and stood right in front of him. Nothing. In a stage whisper: *Jerry! It's me! It's Milberg!* He jumps up from the seat, recognizes me in my robe and medieval apothecary hat. "Milberg!!" he yells, "What are *you* doing here!?" We clinch. I go back to join my children. (I have to say that this difficult man who threw me out of his ballets so many times not only hired me as a principal dancer for his Ballets: USA, but sent me a humongous basket of flowers when my first book was published, with a card saying how proud of me he was!)

By now my kids were really tired of hearing me go on about Wallace Stevens. Sam, the youngest, wrote a poem entitled "Wallace Sneakers," Alex dyed her hair "Cyclamen," a startling hot pink, and Benji disappeared into higher mathematics. Their father had disappeared quite a while before and was engaged on his second unhappy marriage (the third time he lucked out). I worked as an adjunct, taught Freshman Comp at Queens College, at City College, and, simultaneously for two or three semesters, at Rutgers, Newark, and did various odd jobs to help cover the rent. My kids pitched in with the cooking and housework—I mean seriously—and never once complained. Not about that.

The friends I made at graduate school continued to maintain a tight little circle. Kathleen, also a mother, lived with us part of each week during a couple of semesters and cooked fragrant vegetable curries for the family when she wasn't studying. Laury mapped out an elaborate study schedule for the months preceding the Dread Oral Exams (on the oversize pages of a newsprint pad the kids used for drawing) and monitored my progress through that summer. The following year, when she was preparing her dissertation for publication and I was just beginning to write mine, she arranged to have me *and* my children spend the summer in Massachusetts with her and a distinguished academic friend, in a lovely old house near a number of research libraries. This time, I helped with the cooking.

In 1990, after years of part-time teaching, the Stevens book finally came out and I received tenure. Long before, my professors had become my colleagues. I did the usual academic rounds and chores: prepared courses, graded student work, read papers at conventions, published essays in literary journals, participated in committees, reviewed books, directed the Honors Program, chaired a couple of sessions at MLA, wrote recommendations, corralled speakers for our Phi Beta Kappa chapter, did a lot of research, supplied the Wallace Stevens entry for Oxford's *American National Biography*, published another book, this time about the use of pure mathematics in literature, and was upgraded to full professor. By now the kids had all left home and left their cats behind.

The one remaining connection with my dance life was Evil Annie (Ann Crowell Inglis). Our families had spent summers together in Maine. She had seen me through fat years and lean years, through pregnancies and divorce, heavy debt and near despair—as well as through undergraduate and graduate studies, publications, promotions, and affairs of the heart. Once, in a dark time, she presented me with a framed, glassed-in treasure of folk wisdom, neatly cross-stitched by herself: THIS TOO SHALL PASS. When Mr. Balanchine died, in April 1983, it was Annie who called me up

Ann Crowell Inglis ("Evil Annie") at Coral Gables, Florida, before attend-
ing the Tenth Annual Symposium for Medieval, Renaissance and Baroque
Studies at the University of Miami where I presented a paper on "Milton's
Diabolical Calculus" (February 23, 2001). Photo by author.

and said let's go to the funeral together. Lincoln was there. Maria was there. Tanny was there. Jerry was there. Betty and Horgie and Eddie Bigelow. Dancers I'd known, dancers I hadn't seen for decades, dancers I never knew. The Russian Orthodox Church at the corner of Park Avenue and 93rd Street was crowded with mournful theater associates and generations of dancers, from fresh-faced students to aged prima ballerinas. One by one we filed past the bier and took leave of the master. After the service, the casket was brought out to the courtyard and set on a platform between two flights of stone steps, a mimosa tree in full bloom curving toward it.

Annie stayed in touch with everybody. She taught ballet classes in Savannah, had become a Master Gardener and a docent at the Telfair Museum, and she functioned as a sort of Central Intelligence Agency for dancers. Whether they'd been in ballet companies or on Broadway, whether they were still dancing or now teaching, whether they were directing companies or doing choreography, running schools or serving as adjudicators on dance panels, she knew where everybody was and what they were doing, the state of their health and the names of their children. She was the tribal memory. Annie told me what was going on with the people I'd known. She told me about the house the Barnetts had built in the Smokies.

Then one day I get a phone call from North Carolina. "Hello Barbara?" says a warm, distinctly familiar southern voice, "This is Ginger. We're having a little get-together in August—can you come?"

Ballet is perhaps the most fragile art. In 1998, on the fiftieth anniversary of its founding, the New York City Ballet presented an all-Balanchine program which included *Orpheus*, the masterpiece created by Balanchine, Stravinsky, Noguchi, Rosenthal—and us— that had been so breathlessly received at its premiere in 1948. The ballet that proved we were a company capable of greatness, that was at least partly responsible for the transformation of Ballet So-

ciety into New York City's resident company. NYCB was now located at Lincoln Center, and along with the regular audience on
that anniversary night, the house was stocked with generations of
alumnae. We saw the curtain rise, heard the familiar opening bars
of music, and watched the progress of this ballet that so many of
us had performed. *Orpheus* had probably never had such an attentive, informed audience.

Unlike most of the dancers around me, I'd spent the past
quarter-century immersed in academia. The last NYCB production
I'd seen was *Don Quixote*, with Balanchine in the title role and Su-
zanne Farrell as his Dulcinea. On this night, I was dumbfounded
by the production slowly unfolding before my eyes. What had happened to *Orpheus?* Where was its edge-of-the-seat intensity? One or
two of the principals were able to project the ballet's style of movement, but most of the dancers didn't seem to know exactly what
they were about. Why, I thought, would anyone bother to come see
it? The movement was all "flatline." Even the tempi seemed tame.

From the outset I was aware of disturbing lapses and changes.
Soon after the opening section, to cite one instance, during the
passage where the Dark Angel leads the bereft bridegroom into
Hades, the original male leads had tossed the lyre to each other
over distances. You prayed they would catch it. Season after season, you prayed that Moncion and Magellanes wouldn't miss the
object curving through space. On this night I was seeing Noguchi's
beautiful instrument practically *handed* from one to the other. No
chance of a fumble. The thrill that attends a good catch, whether
on the ballfield or in the theater, was gone. Maybe this is trivial, but
I felt a kind of outrage.

There's a phrase dancers use when they see hard steps made
easier, little things left out. In the dialectic of ballet shop talk, they
say the thing has been "watered down." Dancers, like all professional theater folk, are fine-tuned to performances. They know
how neglect of detail or lack of precision can destroy the build-
up of suspense, deaden a whole production. But along with the
general watering down of movement in this production, there was
an astonishing (to me) omission that had nothing to do with the

choreography. On that anniversary night, when the white silk curtain fell at the "second death" of Eurydice, instead of an inert body
pulled swiftly out of sight we saw the dancer scramble to roll behind it. That was not the problem. What surprised me was that the
curtain itself remained motionless. There was no ominous billowing, no cloudlike thrustings from behind to cover the disappearance of the beloved.

I remembered how important that curtain was to Mr. B. I recalled how, just before the premiere, they found that there was no
money to pay for the costly curtain of parachute silk, not a nickel.
How Mr. B was informed at the eleventh hour that he'd have to do
without it. Even Lincoln was unable to meet the cost or raise the
money. The rest is legend. Balanchine told everybody to wait, left
the theater for a few hours and came back, miraculously, with the
necessary amount. He wouldn't say where he got it, or who he'd
touched for it, or what long-standing debt he'd called in, and to my
knowledge nobody ever found out. He never told, but *Orpheus* got
its curtain. At dress rehearsal, Balanchine showed us little Furies,
and some of the stage crew, how to push the thick white silk into
billows from behind as the inert Maria disappeared under it into
darkness. The effect was uncanny, ghostly, marvelous.

These were good dancers we were watching but they desperately
needed prime rehearsal time. With somebody who knew every aspect of the ballet and every step. I have to say, though, that the Bacchantes were terrific that night, every last one of them: sharp, on
the music, intense. They knew, I'll bet, that the original Leader of
the Bacchantes was watching. Tanaquil Le Clercq was taking in the
show, seated in her wheelchair down there in the orchestra aisle. I
came away from that evening saddened, but struck with a revelation. I had never before realized how very good the original company was!

It's August 2004 as I write this and in a few weeks I'll be heading
out to North Carolina to join the old gypsies gathering at the Bar-

netts. It's also about halfway through the Balanchine Centennial year—one hundred years since the birth of Georgi Melitonovitch Balanchivadze on January 22, 1904, in St. Petersburg—and I recently had the singular pleasure of seeing four of his ballets exquisitely danced at ABT's celebration of that event. (American Ballet Theatre, which had long ago premiered that historic *Theme and Variations*, was now performing in the new Metropolitan Opera House at Lincoln Center.) I'd also received announcements since September 2003 from the George Balanchine Foundation and the George Balanchine Trust detailing "Special Presentations, Programs, Symposiums, and Exhibitions" that were planned for the centennial. Performances, talks, interviews, TV presentations, museum showings, library installations, videos, and documentary films had been scheduled. In the States there were coast-to-coast events, everything from Balanchine's Confessor, Father Adrian, who was giving a talk at Harvard University, to seasons devoted wholly to the Balanchine canon. Included were some top-notch American companies: the Pacific Northwest Ballet, the Dance Theatre of Harlem, the Miami City Ballet, and the Pittsburgh and Atlanta Ballets (to name a few directed by dancers I had known personally), and of course the NYCB.

More than sixty ballet companies were observing the centennial in Scandinavia, Germany, Holland, France, Croatia, and Australia. Special all-Balanchine seasons had been put into motion by the Bolshoi and Kirov troupes in Russia, the Paris Opera Ballet, the Royal Ballet in London. At the Hermitage Theatre in St. Petersburg, an elaborate International Symposium, "Balanchine: Past, Present, and Future" was scheduled for June. The activities announced in send-outs from the Balanchine Foundation and Trust between September 2003 and May 2004 covered over thirty closely written pages. As I write, most of these events and performances have already taken place. It looks like Mr. Balanchine's ballets didn't disappear into thin air after all.

In *Balanchine: A Biography*, Bernard Taper recounts a discussion he had with Mr. B concerning the preservation of his works. I heard the familiar response: "For whom?" asks Balanchine. "For

people to see that I don't even know . . . that aren't even born yet?
And are my ballets going to be danced by dancers I don't know,
that I haven't trained? Those won't really be my ballets." His next
comment is thought-provoking, considering the source. "The choreography, the steps—those don't mean a thing" says Balanchine.
"Steps are made by a person. It's the person dancing the steps—
that's what choreography is, not the steps themselves."[6]

How can we know the dancer from the dance? I thought of the
way Mr. B worked with us, at times abandoning the original steps,
shifting into a different mode, altering whole passages to suit a
particular style of movement. Sometimes, though, it seemed that
he just felt like changing a segment, re-energizing it. After all, he
was the choreographer. And he was alert to the changes that inevitably attend new productions of grand old works like *Swan Lake*
and *Sleeping Beauty*. Dance is a living art, not a museum exhibit or
laboratory specimen—a dead butterfly to be preserved in formal-
dehyde. On the other hand, the survival of Balanchine's works was
important to a lot of people, and he knew it.

There was another angle. What he told his dancers was not always what he said to interviewers. He did avow, more than once,
that after he was gone his ballets would fall apart. We all remember that—and to a certain extent he was justified. But Evil Annie
reminded me not too long ago of his other, more positive predic-
tion, also repeated more than once, which suggests precisely the
reverse: "You will all leave me and go and start ballet schools and
companies" he prophesied, "and there will be good dancers all over
America." And isn't that exactly what's happened?

Bobby and Virginia Barnett took charge of the Atlanta Ballet,
the oldest regional company in America. Bobby set eleven Balanchine ballets for their dancers and still teaches classes from Ha-
waii to Alaska. During Balanchine's lifetime, Una Kai was sent
all over the world to stage his ballets; she taught for years at the
Royal Ballet School in Copenhagen, then joined director Todd Bolender as Ballet Mistress of the Kansas City Ballet. Todd produced
many of Balanchine's ballets, staged a number of his own, and
continued to choreograph for that company. The irrepressible Me-

lissa Hayden relocated to Winston-Salem with her husband, and has staged no fewer than fourteen of Mr. B's works for the North Carolina School of the Arts. She continues to teach at that academy, rigorously training her dance students in Balanchine technique. Maria Tallchief remarried twice, started her own school and a brand-new company in Chicago where she not only taught but created her own ballets. Vida Brown, my erstwhile Ballet Mistress *and* Matron of Honor, married a physician, and then an eminent psychologist and moved to Washington, D.C., where she taught for years. Before retiring, she set Balanchine ballets in Italy, Denmark, the Netherlands, and at the Paris Opera. Called out of retirement and working only from notes taken when Mr. B was rehearsing the ballet, she singlehandedly revived *Gounod Symphony* for the San Francisco troupe (and still plays serious golf). Annie Inglis teaches in Savannah and directs student recitals—when she's not digging in the gardens or entertaining a horde of friends. Ronnie Colton and his wife turned the Augusta Ballet into a notable regional company. Barbara Walczak taught for years in New York City, and has compiled a unique collection of Balanchine's classes; while Barbara Horgan, who became Balanchine's personal assistant, is now his watchdog—the honored Trustee who supervises the licensing of Balanchine ballets.

High-flying Patricia Wilde was called to direct the Pittsburgh Ballet in Pennsylvania; the formidable Yvonne Mounsey teaches in California; and Jillana teaches intensive summer courses of Balanchine technique in Taos, New Mexico, both for dance students and for teachers. Roy Tobias, my favorite partner of old, went further afield: after working for years in Tokyo both as Ballet Master and choreographer with four different companies, Roy became the Artistic Director of the Universal Ballet in Korea, then Associate Director of the Seoul Ballet Theater. For the Korean companies, he staged two of Balanchine's most moving ballets—*Serenade* and *La Sonambula*—as well as two of the most difficult, *Apollo,* and *Four Temperaments.* Allegra Kent, who marvelously recreated the title role in *Sonambula* (originally *Night Shadow*), the part danced by Alexandra Danilova, flew out to Seoul to help stage that ballet.

Jacques d'Amboise, who was discovered by Mr. B as a teenager and remained an NYCB star for over thirty years, formed the National Dance Institute—a school and a foundation. He trains teachers to train children, largely boys from diverse backgrounds, without charge. His wife, Carolyn George d'Amboise, blossomed into a gifted photographer after retiring from the company. Eddie Villella's Miami Ballet has developed a reputation for vigor and elegant performances, and anybody remotely connected with dance in America knows that Francia Russell and her husband and co-director, Kent Stowell, have turned the Pacific Northwest Ballet into one of the premier companies in the nation, with particularly fine productions of Balanchine works. Finally, echoing Balanchine's celebrated response to the young Lincoln Kirstein (who was itching to start an American company)—*But first, a school!*—there is Arthur Mitchell's dance academy, and the vital, exciting Dance Theatre of Harlem he nurtured. Arthur and Jacques, Eddie Villella—and Maria Tallchief—have been honored at the Kennedy Center's annual awards—this nation's highest recognition of accomplishment in the arts. This is of course a partial list, a mere fraction, limited to the dancers I knew so long ago.

What critic was it—Northrop Frye?—or perhaps it was W. H. Auden, the poet, who suggested that Prospero's wooden staff would not remain buried, no matter how deep it was planted in the earth? Who came up with the idea that, in time, the magician's wand would put out tiny rootlets, that it would break out of the earth, send up branches and leaves and become a living tree—like the tree that held Ariel prisoner until Prospero set him loose. The theory has a mythic resonance. It calls up the image of the Cosmic Tree rooted deep in the earth with its branches among the stars, or the World Tree, that regenerates after being utterly destroyed by fire. Maybe that's a good figure for Balanchine's teaching taking root, for his dancers starting ballet schools and companies all over America, for his works branching out all over the world, his ballets performed, sending their winged seed aloft to inspire new works. For the works do live, and the revels go on . . . and on . . . and on . . .

Dancers ascending boardwalk at Tybee Island, Georgia (1996). Una Kai (at top) followed in turn by Ann Inglis, Arlouine Case Shaw, and Charlotte Ray Hamer. Photo: Copyright by Carolyn George d'Amboise

Notes

Chapter 3. Introducing Stravinsky

1. Maria Tallchief with Larry Kaplan, *America's Prima Ballerina* (New York: Henry Holt, 1997), 119.
2. Bernard Taper, *Balanchine: A Biography* (New York: Times Books, 1984), 220–21.
3. Ibid., 223.

Chapter 4. Politics

1. Philip Roth, "Communist," *The New Yorker*, August 3, 1998, 60.
2. Taper, *Balanchine*, 213–15.

Chapter 5. An Unexpected Turn

1. The Karsavina photographs referred to are included in "An Album of Nijinsky Photographs," in *Dance Index* 2, no. 3 (March 1943).
2. Arlene Croce, *Going to the Dance* (New York: Knopf, 1982), 20–21.

Chapter 8. On Tour, 1952: A View from the Wings

1. Anatole Chujoy, *The New York City Ballet* (New York: Knopf, 1953), 13.

Chapter 10. The Russian Easter Bribe

1. Chujoy, *New York City Ballet*, 236.

Chapter 11. *Opus 34* and the Loopies

1. The Eakins Press Foundation, *Choreography by George Balanchine: A Catalogue of Works*, rev. ed. (New York: Viking Penguin, Inc., 1984), 210.
2. Edwin Denby, *Dance Writings* (New York: Knopf, 1986), 441–43.

Chapter 12. Mr. B Gets Mad

1. Lawrence Gilman, *New York Herald Tribune*, January 21, 1939.

Chapter 13. Of Rats and Mice and Candy-Canes

1. Taper (quoting Lincoln Kirstein), *Balanchine*, 171.
2. Telephone interview with Ruthanna Boris, May 1, 2005.
3. Tallchief, *America's Prima Ballerina*, 88–89.

Chapter 14. Mostly Mo - tz - art

1. Robert Craft, "Stravinsky and Balanchine," *New York Review of Books*, October 8, 1998.
2. Denby, *Dance Writings*, 300. Denby is discussing Balanchine's approach to his dancers in the Ballet Russe de Monte Carlo (March 23, 1945).

Chapter 15. A Pep Talk

1. John Martin, *New York Times*, March 11, 1954.

Chapter 16. Nightmare in Copenhagen

1. Francis Mason, *I Remember Balanchine: Recollections of the Ballet Master by Those Who Knew Him* (New York: Doubleday, 1991), 186.

Chapter 17. A Class of One's Own

1. Mason, *I Remember Balanchine*, 394.
2. Ibid., 395.
3. Ibid., 35.

Chapter 18. *Agon*: Point Counterpoint

1. Edwin Denby, "Three Sides of 'Agon'" in *Evergreen Review* (Winter 1959); reprinted in Denby, *Dance Writings*, 461.
2. Ibid., 461.
3. Charles M. Joseph, *Stravinsky and Balanchine: A Journey of Invention* (New Haven: Yale University Press, 2002), 247–49.

4. Ibid., 245. Joseph expands here on Stravinsky's minute control of timing in the score: "Beyond matters of pitch control, Stravinsky . . . constantly clocks the individual sections of *Agon* with temporal precision. He fastidiously marks the duration of individual passages in total seconds, sometimes as often as every few measures."

5. Arlene Croce, "The Spelling of Agon" in *The New Yorker*, July 12, 1993, 89.

6. Osip Mandelstam, "Conversation about Dante" in *The Selected Poems of Osip Mandelstam*, tr. Clarence Brown and W. S. Merwin (New York: New York Review Books, 2004), 104. In this essay, Mandelstam explores the poetics of Dante's *Commedia*, rendering the term "instruments" as set forth here not only as producers of musical vibrations but as variations ("transformations") of images.

7. Croce, "Spelling of Agon," 85–86.

Epilogue: *Our revels now are ended*

1. While *The Tempest* is the last play written by Shakespeare alone, he is known to have collaborated on at least two other plays after retiring from the theater.

2. William Shakespeare, *The Tempest*, eds. Virginia Mason Vaughan and Alden T. Vaughan (London: The Arden Shakespeare, third series, 2000), 4.1.418–59.

3. Wallace Stevens, "The Idea of Order at Key West," in *The Collected Poems of Wallace Stevens* (New York: Alfred A. Knopf, 1969), 129.

4. Joan Acocella, "Drastic Classic," *The New Yorker*, March 22, 2004, 99.

5. Stevens, "The Planet on the Table," in *Collected Poems*, 532–33.

6. Taper, *Balanchine*, 321.

Index

Page numbers in *italics* represent illustrations.

205

About the Author

Barbara Milberg Fisher performed and traveled under George Balanchine with Ballet Society and the New York City Ballet from 1946 to 1958, rising to soloist and dancing principal roles. In 1958, she joined Jerome Robbins' newly formed Ballets: USA as one of its principal dancers. She is currently professor emeritus of English at the City College of New York, lives in Manhattan, and remains addicted to baroque music and murder mysteries.